William Macdonald Sinclair

Words to the Laity

William Macdonald Sinclair
Words to the Laity
ISBN/EAN: 9783743338333
Manufactured in Europe, USA, Canada, Australia, Japa
Cover: Foto ©Thomas Meinert / pixelio.de

Manufactured and distributed by brebook publishing software (www.brebook.com)

William Macdonald Sinclair

Words to the Laity

WORDS TO THE LAITY

Addresses and Papers

ON

SUBJECTS OF CONTEMPORARY ECCLESIASTICAL
CONTROVERSY

BY THE

VEN. WILLIAM MACDONALD SINCLAIR, D.D.

ARCHDEACON OF LONDON, CANON OF ST. PAUL'S, EXAMINING CHAPLAIN TO THE
BISHOP OF LONDON, CHAPLAIN-IN-ORDINARY TO H.M. THE QUEEN, AND
FORMERLY SCHOLAR OF BALLIOL COLLEGE, OXFORD

London
JAMES NISBET & CO.
21 BERNERS STREET
1895

TO

HUGH
FIRST DUKE OF WESTMINSTER, K.G.

WITH

PROFOUND ADMIRATION FOR HIS PRINCIPLES
AND CHARACTER

PREFACE

I THINK it is right that those who find in the Church of England, as it was understood from the time of the Reformation till the Counter-Reformation inaugurated by Cardinal Newman, the closest correspondence with Holy Scripture and the Primitive Church which circumstances permit, should be allowed to state their reasons for this opinion without being accused of attacking those who disagree from their view. There is abundance of literature on the other side: perhaps the promoters of the Counter-Reformation may even welcome this little collection of essays and addresses as an exponent of views to which the younger amongst them are unaccustomed. We all have so much in common that it is desirable that we should understand each other, and know where it is that we differ, and why. There need be no acrimony in religious discussion; each side may credit the other with honesty and sincerity. I am in no sense myself a party man; but holding as I do very strongly to the teaching of the great divines of the Church of England, from the Reformers themselves to Waterland, and loving with deep earnestness the simplicity of the reformed English worship, I have no hesitation in stating, as far as I can, the grounds for that adhesion and that affection. The plain Christian teaching which is usually heard from the pulpit of St. Paul's, and the quiet dignity of our Cathedral service, encourage me in the hope that we may all some day return to the great primary verities of Christianity as we find them in the New Testament itself. I have said nothing in breach of charity. May the Holy Spirit grant us a right judgment in all things!

CONTENTS

CHAPTER I.

THE BENEFITS OF THE REFORMATION.

	PAGE
Archbishop Benson on the disparagement of the Reformation	1
Duty of protecting our deliberate opinions	2
The mechanical organisation of Catholicism	2
True and false conceptions of the Church	4
Supremacy of Holy Scripture	5
Repudiation of the Infallibility of the Church	8
Dethronement of Tradition	9
Restoration of the scriptural model of the ministry	10
Return to scriptural view of Lord's Supper	11
Abrogation of unwarranted restrictions	14
Abolition of Imposture	15
No more Intercession of Saints	17
Purification of the lives of the clergy	18
Return to reasonable worship	19
Retention of primitive order	20
Summary	21

CHAPTER II.

THE PRINCIPLES OF THE REFORMATION.

"The Lord's Day and the Holy Eucharist"	22
Results of Dr. Newman's movement	25
The School of the Reformation	27

CONTENTS

	PAGE
Enumeration of thirty-five principles	29
Contemporary clerical opinion	37
Failings of the Reformation School	38
Strength of Dr. Newman's School	39
Impossibility of surrender	41
Summary of Prayer-book teaching on disputed points	42
Importance of understanding fundamentals	44
The Prayer-book arranged by the Reformers	45
The laity not sacerdotal as a whole	46
Wisdom of dropping legal prosecutions	46
Home mission work	47

CHAPTER III.

THE POSITION OF THE LAITY IN THE PRIMITIVE CHURCH.

Ministers the representatives of the whole body	48
Co-ordinate rights of laymen	49
Lay instruction in the assembly	50
Missionary rights of laymen	50
The preaching of Justin Martyr	51
Lay preaching in churches	51
Cause of restrictions	52
Lay Baptism	53
Story by Rufinus	54
Evidence of the Fathers	54
Administration of Holy Communion early restricted	56
Election of ministers	56
Laymen in General Councils	57
Lay Patronage	58
Lay meetings in churches for psalm-singing	58
Conclusion	59

CHAPTER IV.

THE USE AND MEANING OF THE WORD CATHOLIC.

	PAGE
Tendency to accept the Church of Rome as its exponent	61
History of the word	62
Pearson, Field, and Jackson on its use	64
The word inapplicable to most ceremonies	67
As applied to the Church	68
Field's Notes of the Catholic Church	69
Pearson on the Catholic Church	70
Teaching of the Prayer-book	74
Misuse	75
The Prayer-book on Traditions and Ceremonies	76

CHAPTER V.

MEANING AND USE OF THE WORD PROTESTANT.

Use of names: Christian, Catholic	80
Necessity of new description for Reformed Catholicism	81
The Protest of Spires	83
Dividing line in modern Christian thought	85
Adoption of the word by Convocation	85
Constitutional use of the word	86
Field, Laud, Sancroft, Jeremy Taylor, Atterbury, &c.	89
Protestant Catholics	91
Importance of the word to English Christianity	92

CHAPTER VI.

A PLEA FOR FORBEARANCE IN DISAGREEMENT.

Archbishop Tait on proselytising intolerance	95
Personal religious liberty	96
Free ideal of the Christian Church	98

	PAGE
Bishop Lightfoot's view	99
Dean Church on Newman's movement	101
Statistics of Newman's movement	102
Archbishop Tait on Comprehension	103
Practices of Newmanism dependent on toleration	105
Tendency of Newmanism to intolerance	106
Duty of protecting liberty	108
Protestantism a living principle	109
Hooker on non-Episcopal Churches	110
Field, Laud, Cosin, and others on the same	111
The authority of General Councils	113
Doctrine of the English Church on the Eucharist	114
Waterland's teaching on sacrifice	115
Duty of maintaining safeguards	116

CHAPTER VII.

OUR UNHAPPY DIVISIONS.

Sections of Christianity	118
Mutual excommunications	120
Absolute exclusiveness of Rome	121
The Lambeth Conference of 1878 on the same	121
The Lambeth Conference of 1888	122
Romanists in England	123
Relation to Nonconformists	123
Hooker's teaching on the Invisible Church	124
Lessons of the Donatist Schism	126
Difference in Church Government	128
Jewel, Whitgift, Bancroft, Andrewes, Hall, Cosin	130
The policy of Exasperation	131
Policy of Friendliness and Courtesy	134
Social difficulties	135

CHAPTER VIII.

SCHISM.

	PAGE
St. Paul's use of the word	137
Schism at Corinth	138
Schism in the Early Church	141
Bingham on different degrees of Schism	141
Jerome on Schism and Heresy	143
Schisms in the Middle Ages	143
Thomas Aquinas' view of Schism	144
Fortunate position of the English Church	146
The Continental and Scottish reformers desired Episcopacy	147
Baxter on Divisions	151
Bacon on Unity	152
Archdeacon John Sinclair on the Sectarian Spirit	153

CHAPTER IX.

CURRENT FALLACIES IN THE CHURCH.

1. Doctrines to be revealed by the Holy Spirit	156
2. Secret doctrines taught in the Forty Days	159
3. Doctrines too sacred to be mentioned in the Bible	161
4. "Romish" taken to mean only "modern Romish"	163
5. "Catholic"	165
6. Use of dangerous words in a special sense	167
7. Ambiguity of the word "High Church"	168
Duty of the Laity	169

CHAPTER X.

INDEPENDENCE AND RIGHTS OF NATIONAL CHURCHES.

Origin of National Churches	171
Dean Jackson on the independence of Visible Churches	172
Ecclesiastical arrangements in the Roman Empire	173

xiv   CONTENTS

	PAGE
Influence of the Teutonic kingdoms	174
No uniformity of practice in primitive times	176
St. Augustine on the Independence of Churches	176
Bingham on varieties of customs and traditions	180
Instances of divergence	183
The Prayer-book on this point	185
The Prayer-book on Ceremonies	186
Summary of the rights of National Churches	188

CHAPTER XI.

THE PRINCIPLES OF CHURCH MUSIC.

Hymns in Apostolic worship	189
Origin of choral services	190
Difference between cathedrals and parish churches	192
Principles common to all choirs	192
Law of Reverence	193
Prayers in the vestry	193
The General Confession and Lord's Prayer	194
Law of Edification	194
Law of Distinctness	195
Principles special to parish choirs	197
Law of Simplicity	197
Softness	198
Law of Unselfishness	199
Law of Modesty	200
Gratitude to church choirs	201

CHAPTER XII.

FASTING COMMUNION NOT OBLIGATORY.

Floating notions on Fasting Communion	203
St. Augustine's saying	203
Bishop Kingdon on the authority of individual Fathers	204
Mistakes of St. Augustine	205

	PAGE
Errors of his age	205
Necessity of fasting reception not held before fourth century	206
Scriptural practice	206
Change	207
Basil on Fasting Reception	207
St. Chrysostom	208
St. Augustine	209
Early English practices and rules	210
Variety of customs in different churches	211
Difference of circumstances between the civilisation of primitive days and ours	212
Complete abstinence differently understood by the ancients	213
Difference of computation of hours	213
Difference of length of fast	214
Difference of climate	215
Bishop Samuel Wilberforce	215
Result of mediæval restrictions	216
Necessary variations from Rome	217
No law of the English Church on the subject	218
Resolutions of the Bishops of the Southern Province in 1893	219

CHAPTER XIII.

THE SCRIPTURAL VIEW OF HOLY COMMUNION.

Many means of grace	221
Holy Communion in the New Testament	222
The service of edification	222
Change from the Consecrated Meal	223
Our Lord's own meaning	223
No perpetual offering of the sacrifice in heaven	225
Teaching of the English Church	226
Teaching of the Council of Trent	228
Waterland's view of sacrifices	229
English divines on the Lord's presence	229
Hooker	231
St. Augustine, Bishop Beveridge, Waterland	232
Bishop Christopher Wordsworth	233

CHAPTER XIV.

THE INVOCATION OF SAINTS.

	PAGE
One Mediator	234
Christ alone to be worshipped in the Primitive Church	238
The Primitive Church condemned the worship of saints	240
Decadence of the Church in the fourth century	243
Origin of the idea of patron saints	244
Pagan influence on Christianity	246
The Roman doctrines of Development and Accommodation	247

CHAPTER XV.

MITRES.

Male and female adornments	250
Origin of ecclesiastical vestments	250
Revival of the Mitre	251
History of the word	252
Metaphorical head-dress in poetical descriptions of St. John and St. James	252
Rhetorical expressions of Paulinus of Tyre	255
Poetical address by Gregory Nazianzene	255
Description by Ammonianus Marcellinus mistaken	256
The infula	256
Decisive language of Tertullian	258
First indisputable appearance of the mitre in the eleventh century	259

WORDS TO THE LAITY

I.

THE BENEFITS OF THE REFORMATION.

"I am becoming every day a less and less loyal son of the Reformation."—RICHARD HURRELL FROUDE.

His Grace the Archbishop of Canterbury has lately, on two prominent occasions, called attention to the habit of treating the Reformation with disparaging remarks. He has himself reminded us that the Reformation was the greatest event in the history of Christendom since the days of the Apostles. And he has borne emphatic testimony to the fact that the Reformers must always rank amongst the most learned and greatest theologians of any age. I do not think that at the present day the enormous and incalculable benefits of the Reformation are sufficiently studied and understood. It is a hurrying age, and innumerable ideas confront our minds; and it is not everybody who has leisure to think and inquire. It is a time when there is a tendency to consider one set of principles as good as another. The instinct of fair play is a grand characteristic of Englishmen; but it is a travesty of that instinct when it leads you to neglect your own principles in favour of those of other bodies antagonistic to your own. It is an abuse of that liberal habit of mind when it makes you disparage facts and influences which have been a power for good in the history of your country which is beyond all estimation.

It is not my habit to reflect on anybody, whether in the Church of Rome or outside of it. Everybody has the right to believe as he pleases, and to express his belief; but sometimes the recognition of that liberty of conscience and of prophesying is taken to imply that everybody has the right except ourselves. The phrase, "I have as much right to my opinion as you," is sometimes used as if it meant, "I may say what I think, but if you do the same I shall consider it an attack on myself." Now, I think the time has come when through the length and breadth of the country—north, south, east, and west—all to whom the Reformation is a priceless boon should speak out with perfect calmness and moderation, and give the reasons for that ineradicable opinion, for which they have the highest authority, and from which they will never part.

The effect of the Reformation in England was not merely the repudiation of the authority of the Western Patriarch; it was a breaking away from the superannuated and darkened theory of the mechanical Catholic Church as it was then understood.[1] The development

[1] Hooker, *Eccl. Pol.*, v. 68, 6. Comp. Bp. Harold Browne, XXXIX. Articles, on Article XIX. and Boultbee's XXXIX. Articles, p. 159, &c.

THE BENEFITS OF THE REFORMATION

of the hierarchy hitherto had been perfectly regular and by orderly stages. The bishoprics had gradually been united under metropolitans, and the metropolitans under patriarchs. There were the Patriarchs of Jerusalem, Alexandria, Antioch, Rome, and Constantinople. The Eastern Churches had in time broken off from the Western, and at last, when they were unable to accept the article of the Nicene Creed, which speaks of the Spirit as proceeding from the Son, an article produced at the Western Council of Aix-la-Chapelle in 809, and condemned by the Eastern Council of Constantinople, the eighth at that city, in 879, then the split on this and on other grounds became definite.[1] Amongst the other grounds for the great disruption were the increasing encroachments of the Western Patriarch on the liberties of other Churches, and his claims for a universal supremacy, first as Bishop of the ancient capital of the Roman Empire, and afterwards as the supposed successor of St. Peter. Some of the Western Churches remonstrated at different times against these encroachments; in particular the Churches of Spain, France, and England. But in the end they submitted. At the time of the Reformation there was nothing different in relationship to Rome between the Church of England and the other national Churches outside

---

[1] Compare Scudamore's *Notit. Euchar.*, 2nd ed., p. 283; Liddon in the *Report of the Bonn Conference*, 1875, p. xxvii.; Ffoulkes, "The Church's Creed and the Crown's Creed."

Italy which had succumbed to the exaggerated and overgrown jurisdiction of the Western Patriarch. At the Reformation the English nation decided that in the arrangements of patriarchates there was nothing essential to the constitution of Christendom. And as the Western Patriarchate had become exceedingly corrupt in doctrine, and refused to recognise the return to primitive principles promoted by the Reformation, it was necessary to fall back on the principle of National Churches, and to break entirely with Rome.

But, besides this act of independence, the Reformation gave us a true instead of a false conception of the Church.[1] Contrary to the language of the New Testament, where a Church always includes the unofficial members as well as their ministers, in the mediæval ages the Church had come to mean a hierarchy with a commission handed down from generation to generation, in communion with one visible centre and authority, having branches in different countries, and with power to alter doctrines and practices in accordance with a belief that it was directly inspired so to act. For this wholly unscriptural ideal the Reformation gave us the true and majestic conception that "the visible Church of Christ is a congregation of faithful men, in the which the pure Word of God is preached, and the Sacraments be duly

[1] Compare Moule, "Outlines of Christian Doctrine," p. 202, and Hooker, *Eccl. Pol.*, Bk. iii.

administered according to Christ's ordinance in all those things that of necessity are requisite to the same." And in the Fifty-fifth Canon we get this definition of Christ's Holy Catholic Church: "That is, the whole congregation of Christian people dispersed throughout the whole world." And in the Prayerbook: "We pray for the good estate of the Catholic Church . . . that all who profess and call themselves Christians may be led into the way of truth, and hold the faith in unity of spirit, in the bond of peace, and in righteousness of life."

Thirdly, the Reformation restored the supremacy of Holy Scripture as the rule of faith. It is the fashion to say that the Church presents the doctrine and that the Bible is used to prove it. That is not the doctrine either of Scripture, or of the Apostles, or of the Fathers, or of the Reformation. Scripture is supreme because it contains the words of Christ Himself, and the words of inspired men. The Fathers after the time of the Apostles drew the sharpest possible distinction between their own words and those of the inspired writers; and when it began to be the custom to draw up formularies at Councils, the Council did not prepare a doctrine and then bring Scripture to prove it, but it deduced the doctrine from the very Scripture itself. In the Book of Homilies it is said: "Let us diligently search for the well of life in the books of the New and Old Testaments, and not run to the stinking puddles of men's traditions, deceived by men's imaginations, for our justification and salvation. For in Holy Scripture is fully contained what we ought to do, and what to eschew, what to believe, what to love, and what to look for at God's hands at length. . . . If it shall require to teach any truth, or reprove false doctrine, to rebuke any vice, to commend any virtue, to give good counsel, to comfort or to exhort, or to do any other thing requisite for our salvation, all those things, saith St. Chrysostom, we may learn plentifully from the Scripture. There is, saith Fulgentius, abundantly enough both for men to eat and for children to suck. There is whatsoever is meet for all ages, and for all degrees and sorts of men. . . . Whosoever giveth his mind to Holy Scripture, with diligent study and burning desire, it cannot be, saith St. John Chrysostom, that he should be left without help. For either God Almighty will send him some godly doctor to teach him—as He did to instruct the eunuch . . . or else, if we lack a learned man to instruct and teach us, yet God Himself from above will give light unto our minds, and teach us those things which be necessary for us, and wherein we be ignorant. And in another place St. Chrysostom saith that man's human or worldly wisdom and science is not needful to the understanding of Scripture; but the revelation of the Holy Ghost, who inspireth the true meaning unto them that with humility and diligence do search therefor." And in confirmation of this great primary view we may remember that the vast majority of Christians agree in plain, simple, fundamental truths: the Fatherhood of God, the Divinity of our Lord, the work of the Holy Spirit, the redemption of the world, the initial rite of baptism, the spiritual festival of the Lord's Supper, the immortality of the soul, the power of prayer, the future reward and punishment, and the like. It is the exception when, in consequence of some strong individual leadership in a different direction, they take a line contrary to any of these primary verities. And so we hold fast as the very palladium of our spiritual liberties the Sixth Article: "Holy Scripture containeth all things necessary to salvation; so that whatever is not read therein, nor may be proved thereby, is not to be required of any man, that it should be received as an article of the faith, or be thought requisite or necessary to salvation." Before the Reformation the old mediæval Church was practically a Church without a Bible; a very large number even of the priests could not read it; to the people it was a sealed book.[1] The Reformation, aided by printing, put the Bible into the hands of the people, drew certain simple summaries of its teaching, and left it to the consciences of the people to apply them to their souls. They did not at once see the full results of the principle of the Liberty of Conscience; these would only be arrived at gradually in the

---

[1] On going to the diocese of Gloucester Bishop Hooper found that out of 311 clergy, 168 were unable to repeat the Ten Commandments, 31 could not say in what part of Scripture they were to be found, 40 could not tell where the Lord's Prayer was written, and 31 did not know who was its author.

emancipation of Nonconformists, the enfranchisement of Roman Catholics, the removal of disabilities from the Jews; but they were inherent in the principle, and their full declaration was only a question of time.

A fourth great gift of the Reformation was the repudiation of the principle of the Infallibility of the Church. Hitherto, whatever the Bishops declared to be true must be accepted without question. The English Church at the Reformation took the more modest view of the Apostles themselves: "As the Church of Jerusalem, Alexandria, and Antioch have erred, so also the Church of Rome hath erred, not only in their living and manner of ceremonies, but also in matters of faith." No ecclesiastical authority could be greater than that of General Councils, which were as far as possible supposed to be representative of the whole Episcopate. Yet about their authority our Church is no less definite in its limitation: "General Councils . . . when they be gathered together (forasmuch as they be an assembly of men, whereof all be not governed with the Spirit and Word of God), they may err, and sometimes have erred, even in things pertaining unto God. Wherefore, things ordained of them as necessary to salvation have neither strength nor authority, unless it may be declared that they be taken out of Holy Scripture."

A fruitful source of error in the mediæval Church was the importance ascribed to Tradition.[1] Nobody

[1] Hooker, *Eccl. Pol.*, i. 14, 5.

might be able to tell how a tradition had originated. But if it was there, it was to be accepted without question. It is easy to see how dangerous an element this must be where the supreme authority of Holy Scripture was not maintained, and how antagonistic that principle must be to Tradition where it was once declared. The unreformed mediæval Church of the West subsequently enshrined the equal authority of tradition with that of Holy Scripture in the decrees of the Council of Trent. Borrowing from that unreformed opinion, members of our Church sometimes in the present day say, "The Church possesses the authentic Catholic tradition, and by this interprets Scripture. A part of this tradition is the authenticity of Holy Scripture, which is therefore received at the hands of the Church, and because we believe the Church. Further, private persons may not search Scripture independently of external help."[1] The Article on the Supremacy of Holy Scripture will not allow this view, which is an exaggeration of the truth. In the mind of the Reformation the Church is "Testis et Conservatrix" of Holy Scripture. She is not the judge, far less the giver, of Scripture. From age to age she has witnessed to each successive generation, "These are the books which I have received, and these I have sedulously preserved." To this I would add the words of Hooker: "The schools of Rome teach Scripture to

[1] Goode's "Divine Rule of Faith and Practice," chap. ii.; Boultbee, XXXIX. Articles, p. 173.

be insufficient, as if, except traditions were added, it did not contain all revealed and supernatural truth, which absolutely is necessary for the children of men in this life to know that they may in the next be saved." The Thirty-fourth Article sets traditions aside—"It is not necessary that traditions and ceremonies be in all places one or utterly alike, for at all times they have been divers, and may be changed according to the diversity of countries, times, and men's manners, so that nothing be ordained against God's Word."

A sixth blessing of the Reformation was the restoration of the Scriptural model of the Christian ministry.[1] Before the unsealing of the Word of God, all men held that the officers of the Church were a sacerdotal caste, like that of the Jews, and that every presbyter was a sacrificing priest. The clergy literally held in their hands the keys of the kingdom of heaven. They were mediators between God and man. Every time they said Mass they repeated the miracle of the Incarnation; and the more often Christ was embodied and offered on the altars, so much the better for the benefit of all present. The priest could cause the shortening of the time of a soul in purgatory by repeating masses on its behalf. All this was not only contrary to the language of Scripture, but it had the worst effect upon the men themselves. They became tyrants, they interfered in everything, they often lost humility,

---

[1] Bishop Lightfoot, *Epistle to the Philippians*, "The Christian Ministry," p. 184, &c.

self-control, honesty, and morality. The Reformation stripped the ministry of its sacerdotal character. The Reformers cast out the words "sacrifice" and "altar" in reference to the Lord's Supper and the Holy Table. They retained the word "priest" when it was necessary to distinguish him from the deacon, but in the original and Scriptural sense of presbyter or elder, not of sacrificer.[1] "They taught the people everywhere that the clergy were not the lords of God's heritage, but, like St. Paul and St. Timothy, its servants, ambassadors, messengers, witnesses, evangelists, teachers, and ministers of the Word and Sacraments." They showed in the Ordination Services that the business of the Presbyterate was not to offer up Christ, but "to be messengers, watchmen, and stewards of the Lord; to teach and to premonish, to feed and provide for the Lord's family; to seek for Christ's sheep that are dispersed abroad, and for His children who are in the midst of this naughty world, that they may be saved through Christ for ever."

A seventh gift of the Reformation was the return to the Scriptural view of the Lord's Supper. The teaching of the corrupt mediæval Church was thus

---

[1] "Whether we call it a Priesthood, a Presbytership, or a Ministry, it skilleth not: though in truth the word *Presbyter* doth seem more fit, and in propriety of speech more agreeable than *Priest*, with the drift of the whole Gospel of Jesus Christ. . . . The Holy Ghost throughout the body of the New Testament making so much mention of them, doth not anywhere call them Priests."—Hooker, *Eccl. Pol.*, v. 78, 3.

subsequently set forth by the Council of Trent: "Since the same Christ, Who once offered Himself by His blood on the Cross, is contained in this Divine sacrifice, which is celebrated in the Mass and offered without blood, the Holy Scripture teaches us that this sacrifice is really propitiatory, and made by Christ. . . . For assuredly God is appeased by this oblation . . . for the sacrifice which is now offered by the ministry of the priests is one and the same as that which Christ there offered on the Cross, only the mode of offering it is different." The doctrine of the Church of England is very simple and direct: "The offering of Christ once made is that perfect redemption, propitiation, and satisfaction for all the sins of the whole world, both original and actual; and there is none other satisfaction for sin but that alone. Wherefore the sacrifices of Masses, in the which it was commonly said that the priest did offer Christ for the quick and the dead, to have remission of pain or guilt, were blasphemous fables and dangerous deceits." And in the Communion Office we speak of Christ, "Who by His one oblation of Himself once offered made there a full, perfect, and sufficient sacrifice, oblation, and satisfaction for the sins of the whole world; and did institute, and in His holy Gospel command us to continue a perpetual memory of that His precious death until His coming again." And in the Catechism: "Why was the Sacrament of the Lord's Supper ordained? For the continual remembrance of the sacrifice of the death of Christ, and of the benefits which we receive thereby." The special presence of our Lord, which we all desire and to which we all cling, is promised in the faithful use of the Lord's Supper, not locally in the bread and wine. As our great divine Hooker has said,[1] "<u>The real presence of Christ's most blessed body and blood is not to be sought in the Sacrament, but in the worthy receiver of the Sacrament.</u> . . . I see not which way it should be gathered by the words of Christ when and where the bread is His body and the cup His blood; but only in the very heart and soul of him who receiveth them. As for the Sacraments, they really exhibit, but, for aught we can gather out of that which is written of them, they are not really, nor do really contain in themselves, that grace which, with them or by them, it pleaseth God to bestow." That is the meaning of another sentence in the Article: "The body of Christ is given, taken, and eaten in the Supper only after an heavenly and spiritual manner. And the mean whereby the body of Christ is eaten and received in the Supper is faith." That is the meaning also of the answer in the Catechism, "The body and blood of Christ are verily and indeed taken and received by the *faithful* in the Lord's Supper." The means of receiving is faith; those who receive them are those who have faith. Those who "be void of a lively faith, although they do carnally and visibly press with their teeth the

[1] Hooker, *Eccl. Pol.*, v. 67, 6.

Sacrament of the body and blood of Christ, yet in nowise are they partakers of Christ, but rather to their condemnation do eat and drink the sign or sacrament of so great a thing."

Again, in pre-Reformation days the Sacrament was superstitiously hedged round by all kinds of restrictions—obligatory fasting, penance, confession and absolution, and the like. These restrictions also, as far as they were considered necessities, the Reformation swept aside. What is required of them who come to the Lord's Supper? says the Catechism. "To examine themselves, whether they repent them truly of their former sins; steadfastly purposing to lead a new life; have a lively faith in God's mercy through Christ, with a thankful remembrance of His death; and to be in charity with all men." Fasting before Communion may be good for some; but, as the Bishops of our Province only last year declared, it is a matter of Christian liberty. If any cannot by self-examination quiet his own conscience, but further requireth comfort or counsel, he is at full liberty to come to his parish clergyman, or to some other discreet and learned minister of God's Word, and open his grief; that by the ministry of God's Word he may receive the benefit of absolution, together with ghostly counsel and advice, to the quieting of his conscience, and avoiding of all scruple and doubtfulness. Our Church prefers self-examination; but in cases where peace cannot be obtained, resort may be had to advice and to instruc-

THE BENEFITS OF THE REFORMATION 15

tion in those parts of God's Holy Word which specially console and assure His forgiveness to all those who truly repent and believe. The old system of obligatory auricular confession was entirely set aside. No institution of the unreformed Catholic Church had a more corrupting or degrading influence.[1] By it the priests interfered "between husbands and wives, between parents and children, between masters and servants, between landlords and tenants, between subjects and sovereigns, between souls and God," in every conceivable relation of life. When carried to its full extent it ended in the poisonous and immoral system of indulgences. It was used for two great objects: enriching the Church and promoting the sacerdotal power. The rescue of souls from purgatory, the enriching of the shrines of favourite saints, the endowment by the dying of abbeys, monasteries, and chapters with vast tracts of land to atone for evil life, led to such a state of things that in fact, says Burnet, if some laws had not restrained them the greater part of all the estates in England had been given to religious houses. The increase of power came by the same means. Absolution was necessary to Communion, Extreme Unction to salvation. To please the priests was the first of duties; they were sacred persons, and for a long time had laws of their own. Fuller, the historian, tells us "that in 1489 a certain Italian priest got an immense sum of money in

[1] Bishop Ryle's "What do we owe to the Reformation?" p. 7.

England by obtaining power from the Pope to absolve people from usury, theft, manslaughter, fornication, and all crime whatsoever, except smiting the clergy and conspiring against the Pope" (Fuller, "Church History," i. 532).

Amongst innumerable other advantages which we owe to the Reformation we must place in the next place the freedom from imposture.[1] Before that era of light the worship of relics and images was universal. You may read about them in Strype, Fuller, and Burnet. At Reading they had an angel with one wing, the spear-head which pierced our Saviour's side, two pieces of the holy cross, St. James's hand, St. Philip's stole, a bone of Mary Magdalene, a bone of Salome. At Bury St. Edmund's were exhibited the coals that roasted St. Lawrence, the parings of St. Edmund's toe-nails, Thomas à Becket's penknife and boots, and as many pieces of our Saviour's cross as would have made when put together one large whole cross. At Maiden Bradley the objects of reverence were the Virgin Mary's smock, a piece of the stone on which our Lord was born at Bethlehem, and a part of the bread used by Christ and the Apostles at the Last Supper. At Bruton, in Somerset, was a girdle of the Virgin in red silk, used in child-births. At Farley Abbey, in Wiltshire, they used a white girdle of St. Mary Magdalene. At St. Mary's Nunnery, in Derby, the Nuns had a piece of St. Thomas's shirt,

[1] Bishop Ryle, p. 8; Strype, i. 390; Burnet, "Reformation," i. 486.

worshipped by women expecting confinement. At Dale Abbey, near Derby, they worshipped part of another girdle of the Virgin Mary, and some of her milk. At Repton the bell of St. Guthlac was in great honour, and those with headache used to put their heads under it. At Grace Dieu, in Leicestershire, they worshipped the girdle and part of the coat of St. Francis. At Hales, in Gloucestershire, a vial was shown on great occasions which was said to contain the blood of Christ. On examination by the Royal Commissioners of Henry VIII., it was found to contain the blood of a duck, renewed every week. At Worcester, in one of the churches, was a huge image of the Virgin, covered with a veil, which on inquiry was found to be the statue of an old Bishop. At Boxley a crucifix was shown which, when copper was offered to it, looked grave; when silver, it relaxed its severity; when gold, it smiled. On examination it was found to be worked by wires. To such a low ebb had religion sunk when the Bible was kept from the people. The boast of the unreformed Western Church is that it is always the same; and these absurdities may be matched on the Continent to this day.

Yet another boon was of immense importance. It was the shattering of the superstition of calling on saints for their prayers. Of course a moment's reasoning reflection will show that the saints, however blessed, are not omnipresent; and, without some such Divine attribute, they could not possibly hear the prayers of their numerous votaries all over the world. But even if they could, the practice would be superstitious. The love of our Lord is perfect, complete, and absolute, and any intercession of His mercy, after all the assurances that He has given us, would be an impiety and an impertinence—"Lo, I am with you alway, even unto the end of the world;" "Him that cometh unto Me I will in nowise cast out."

The Reformation purified the lives of the clergy, and restored the universal obligation of the strictest Christian morality. The lives of the clergy and the monks were the scandal of Christendom. Here and there faithful religious houses might be found, and pious clergy; but the open immorality of the conduct of most was the subject of common satire. The Western Churches had themselves aimed at reform, but to be reformed the clergy refused. The terrible system of casuistry, or setting forth rules for cases of conscience, had provided excuses for the breach of every commandment, and the practical divorce between faith and morality was complete. That faith without morality is dead is a revived doctrine of the New Testament, which is not the least of the gifts we owe to the Reformation. To the influence and example of the Reformation, even the unreformed Western Catholic Church is itself indebted; there have been fewer Popes of notorious and scandalous wickedness, and the Romish priesthood has been far more consistent and careful than before. In England they conform as much as possible to the lives and manners of the best of the reformed clergy.

The Reformation gave us a reasonable and intelligible system of public worship. When Romanism was prevalent and undisturbed, all services must have been mysterious performances undertaken by the priest on behalf of the people in a foreign tongue and in unintelligible tones. The Reformers not only gave us the English Bible and the English Prayer-book, but they placed the service of edification, described by St. Paul in the Epistle to the Corinthians,[1] side by side with the service of the Lord's Supper, and they raised the office of instruction and preaching to the dignity with which it had been endowed by St. Paul. They restored the liberty of National Churches to settle their own ceremonies, and made the services as simple as they could possibly be. "Every particular or National Church hath authority to ordain, change, and abolish ceremonies or rites of the Church ordained only by man's authority, so that all things be done to edifying." None were to bring back ceremonies not authorised by the provisions of the National Church; the sole book of ordinances was the Book of Common Prayer and Administration of the Sacraments, and other rites and ceremonies according to the use of the Church of England. "The particular forms of Divine worship, and the rites and ceremonies to be used therein, being things in their own nature indifferent, and

[1] 1 Cor. xiv. 23.

alterable, and so acknowledged, it is but reasonable that upon weighty and important considerations, according to the exigency of times and occasions, such changes and alterations should be made therein as to those that are in place of authority, should from time to time seem necessary or expedient." "The godly and decent order of the ancient Fathers had been altered, broken, or neglected . . . with multitude of responds, verses, vain repetitions, commemorations, and synodals." All henceforth was to be simple and easily understood by the people. The Romish mitre was discarded. The Romish vestments were cut up to make table "carpets," hangings for the pulpit, and in cathedrals sometimes to form copes. At St. Paul's Cathedral, the Dean and Chapter begged thirty albs out of the spoil to make surplices for the ministers and choristers.[1] The plain white surplice, a quiet and primitive costume, became the dress for all the ministrations of the Church. Public worship was made an exercise for the mind and reason as well as for the heart.

I might mention many other particular privileges which we owe to the Reformation. It kept for us the old primitive order of Church government, for which we cannot be too thankful as a starting-point for the future reform and reunion of the Christian Churches. But it ranges together side by side in defence of light and liberty, all Christian Churches

[1] Dugdale, *Hist.* App. p. 58.

and bodies who hold the primitive faith of the Gospels. Some may be more perfect in organisation; some may be, through the necessary misfortunes of history, defective; but all alike we are excommunicated by the unreformed Churches of the Western Patriarchate, and all alike we have the perpetual duty to protest against that excommunication, and the errors, superstitions, and unscriptural developments to which it is due.

Such was the Reformation. It found darkness, corruption, and tyranny; it gave us light, morality, and liberty. It restored the Bible to its position as the rule of faith. It recovered for the laity the place which they had lost. It revived learning throughout Europe. It appealed to Scriptures and to the witness of the Primitive Church. It reunited faith and holiness. It opened once more the freedom of access of the soul to Christ for pardon and peace. No human movement is perfect; no human composition is free from error; but the teaching of the Church of England in Articles and Prayer-book in its simple, plain historical sense, is to our minds as near the mind of the Apostles as human documents can be made. The liberty and purity of the English Church have made England great; and, please God, we will support that liberty and purity with all our hearts and minds and souls as the secret of the happiness and prosperity of our people.

II.

THE PRINCIPLES OF THE REFORMATION: THEIR PROSPECTS AT THE PRESENT DAY.

"I have long been convinced that there is nothing in the Council of Trent which could not be explained satisfactorily to us, if it were to be explained authoritatively. . . . This involves the conviction that there is nothing in our Articles which cannot be explained rightly as not contradicting anything to be held *de fide* in the Roman Catholic Church."—Dr. PUSEY.[1]

THERE is nothing gained by concealing from ourselves that there are at the present day, amongst the various divisions of the clergy, two great schools of thought living side by side and intermingling in every direction within the organisation known as the Church of England. One would properly be called Sacerdotal, or Mediæval; the other Primitive, or Reformed. The terms High Church and Low Church have nothing whatever to do with the distinctions between them, and are altogether misleading. The "Broad" Church is now so much mixed up with the "High" in ceremonial and Biblical criticism, and coheres so little together, that it need not here be reckoned. The subject can be discussed with perfect good-temper and

[1] Letter to the *Tablet*, Nov. 22, 1865.

unreserved freedom, for all of us have intimate associates on both sides. The laymen of the time do not, to any great extent, enter into the controversies that have been raised, nor do the mass of them understand the issues. The laymen, for the most part, are content with a very plain, simple, and Scriptural type of Christianity. There is every indication that if they could be polled, or if they could be roused to exercise any distinct influence in the affairs of the Church, they would be found in an overwhelming degree on the side of the principles that are Primitive, Reformed, or Evangelical. In discussing points of difference it is well to remember that it is mainly, at present, a concern of the clergy. Both sets are ordained by the same bishops; but while the one set believe that they are accepting no authority or directions except those of the Prayer-book, the others consider that there is a great undefined body behind the Prayer-book called the Catholic Church, to which they owe an equal or superior allegiance, an undefined set of opinions and practices called by them "Catholic Tradition," which it is their business to teach and to employ. For the moral effects of the Reformation they are grateful; but there is much in it which they openly and sincerely deplore. In their latest manifesto ("The Lord's Day and the Holy Eucharist") they explain with great frankness some of the changes which they desire. These are many and important: the alteration of the Communion Office, to make it resemble the mediæval

Use of Sarum, which is the object of their affectionate and regretful admiration; the stamping of the Church of England once for all with the sacerdotal idea; the reservation of the elements used in Holy Communion; the restoration of the Mass and the like. "When, indeed,"[1] writes Lord Halifax, in a burst of candour, speaking of English Cathedrals, "shall we see the altars restored in the side-chapels, constant services with throngs of worshippers throughout all the early hours of the morning, and a Chapter Eucharist sung at nine o'clock after the office of the day has been said, as a regular matter of course? In view of all that has been accomplished during the last fifty years, nothing is impossible. Let us not despair, then, even of such a change as this; the opportunities that are being vouchsafed to the Church of England are indeed wonderful." "Weekly attendance at Mass,"[2] writes another in the same volume, "regular instruction, Communion at Easter, and perhaps at Whitsuntide and Christmas—that should be the rule to aim at for all as a minimum. For the majority, also, it will be the safest maximum." "Why," writes another, "change the title? why reject the old and certainly inoffensive term 'the Mass'? . . . The aim of modern 'Ritualism' has been simply to restore so much of the old ritual as seemed absolutely necessary for the reverent and Catholic celebration of the Eucharist."[3]

[1] "The Lord's Day and the Holy Eucharist," p. 38.
[2] Ibid. p. 94.   [3] Ibid. p. 121.

"Mankind,"[1] writes Lord Halifax, "in its present condition can be no more dispensed from the necessity of expiation than it can from the necessity of love and obedience . . . we are bound to expiate as far as we can." "The entrance of the high-priest,"[2] writes Dr. Linklater, "into the Holy of Holies on the day of atonement with the blood of the victim, we are told in the New Testament, was the type of the entrance of our great High Priest, Jesus Christ, with His own blood into heaven itself, there to appear before the presence of God for us. That is what He is doing in heaven for us . . . and He has told us to 'do' on earth at the earthly altar what He is 'doing' in heaven at the altar there. The Jewish priest had nothing better than a poor little lamb to represent this. God puts into the hands of the Christian priest the adorable mystery of the Blessed Sacrament—the Body and the Blood—that we may lift it up and offer it to God." "We know,"[3] writes Mr. Going, "that in this Blessed Sacrament He has fulfilled His word, 'Lo, I am with you alway, even unto the end of the world,' and we will worship and adore Him where we know we can always find Him, viz., in the Blessed Sacrament of the Altar."

The excellent, earnest, zealous, and self-sacrificing men who, following the teaching of Dr. Newman, and especially of Tract XC., have adopted such opinions

---

[1] "The Lord's Day and the Holy Eucharist," p. 4.
[2] Ibid. p. 169.   [3] Ibid. p. 220.

and have such objects in view, are now exceedingly numerous, and increase in number every year. There are already more than 1000 churches in England where the mediæval eucharistic vestments, the symbol of the sacerdotal doctrine, are worn. Many practices, abrogated at the English Reformation, are being revived: prayers and masses for the dead, invocation of the Virgin and Saints, withholding the cup from the laity, omission or mumbling of half the words of administration, insistence on fasting communion, insistence on auricular confession, the employment of the Use of Sarum simultaneously with the Communion Office, or in its place. In some places even the cultus of painted images has been restored; in some, that of the Sacred Heart; in others, that of pieces of the True Cross. The clergymen of whom we are speaking have recommended themselves by their active work amongst the poor. A still larger number of clergymen hold more or less of their special opinions, though they do not go the length of wearing the vestments, which have been pronounced contrary to the existing law. A number of the clerical seminaries, which prepare young men for orders, are understood to sympathise, more or less, with the revived sacerdotal theology, without going to what are called extreme lengths. Seven of the august and exalted Prelates of English sees have shown a visible encouragement for these excellent men by wearing the obsolete mitre, which was discarded at the Reformation as a symbol of the unreformed Church. The old-fashioned High Church clergymen give the men of the movement the countenance of their friendly indulgence. The influence of the movement in the press is enormous; it has some of the ablest reviews and journals. One of their organs, in a retrospect of the extraordinary change which has taken place during the last half century, is perhaps justified in its exultant prophecy that when another fifty years have passed the mediæval vestments will be worn and the mediæval doctrine taught in every parish in the Church of England. Holy Scripture will no longer be the supreme rule of faith. <u>The inspired Church which provided the Bible will be its sole authoritative interpreter.</u> The representatives of the theology and history of the National Church during the last three centuries and a half will, according to this view, if not altogether extinct, be reduced to a small and insignificant set of eclectic and pedantic purists.

The other prominent school of the clergy represents Primitive or what are known as Reformation principles. They may be roughly described as those who believe the English Reformation, as represented in the Prayer-book and Articles of the English Church, to have arrived as nearly as may be at the mind of the Apostolic and sub-Apostolic ages. They do not regard the Reformers as having any absolute authority like that ascribed to Popes or to inspired teachers; but they hold that the Reformation was a tremendous and almost unique crisis, and that the subjects in dispute were then thoroughly sifted and the conclusions obtained satisfactory. They do not mean that any mere human set of statements, ranging over a vast variety of matters of the greatest importance, is incapable of improvement; but they consider that the attempt to alter them would let loose such a turbulent flood of discord that the small possible gain would be infinitely overbalanced by the seas of trouble which would follow. And they gladly recognise the close and accurate correspondence between the documents to which they have sworn allegiance and the language of Scripture and of the really Primitive Church. They see no reason whatever for altering the principles on which, in accordance with that really Primitive Church, the National Communion has rested for three centuries and a half, and under which the country has grown free and great; and although they are anxious to live at peace with all men, and to tyrannise over no man's conscience, they can find no conceivable ground for altering these principles in order to accommodate what appears to them the ill-omened desire of pious men to revert to the times of darkness and superstition. In all quietness and modesty they hold to their own opinions.

What, then, are these English Reformation principles? It would be, of course, impossible to set them forth at length, or with scientific precision, in the limits of a brief article; but they can be indicated with sufficient clearness in the phraseology of the Prayer-book and Articles.

THE PRINCIPLES OF THE REFORMATION

1. *Supreme authority of Scripture.*[1]

Holy Scripture containeth all things necessary to salvation; so that whatever is not read therein, nor may be proved thereby, is not to be required of any man, that it should be believed as an article of the Faith, or be thought requisite or necessary for salvation.

2. *Acceptance of the Three Creeds.*[2]

The Three Creeds ... ought thoroughly to be received and believed: for they may be proved by most certain warrants of Holy Scripture.

3. *Justification by Faith.*[3]

We are accounted righteous before God only for the merit of our Lord and Saviour Jesus Christ by faith.

4. *The Definition of the Visible Church.*[4]

The visible Church of Christ is a congregation of faithful men, in the which the pure Word of God is preached, and the Sacraments be duly administered according to Christ's ordinance in all those things that of necessity are requisite to the same.

5. *Definition of the Catholic Church.*[5]

We pray for the good estate of the Catholic Church ... that all who profess and call themselves Christians may be led into the way of truth, and hold the faith in unity of spirit, in the bond of peace, and in righteousness of life.

6. *The Church not infallible.*[6]

As the Church of Jerusalem, Alexandria, and Antioch have erred, so also the Church of Rome hath erred, not only in their living and manner of ceremonies, but also in matters of Faith.

General Councils ... when they be gathered together (forasmuch as they be an assembly of men, whereof all be not governed with the Spirit and Word of God), they may err, and sometimes

---

[1] Article VI.   [2] Article VIII.   [3] Article XI.   [4] Article XIX.
[5] Prayer for all conditions of men.   [6] Articles XIX. and XXI.

have erred, even in things pertaining unto God. Wherefore things ordained of them as necessary to salvation have neither strength nor authority, unless it may be declared that they be taken out of Holy Scripture.

7. Orders.

It is not lawful for any man to take upon him the office of public preaching, or ministering the Sacraments in the Congregation, unless he be lawfully called and sent to execute the same. And those we ought to judge lawfully called and sent, which be chosen and called to this work by men who have public authority given unto them in the Congregation to call and send Ministers into the Lord's vineyard.

8. The Orders of an Episcopal Church.

It is evident unto all men diligently reading the Holy Scripture and ancient authors, that from the Apostles' time there have been these Orders of Ministers in Christ's Church; Bishops, Priests, and Deacons. . . . To the intent that these Orders may be continued, and reverently used and esteemed in the Church of England: no man shall be accounted or taken to be a lawful Bishop, Priest, or Deacon in the Church of England, or suffered to execute any of the said functions, except he be called, tried, examined, and admitted thereunto according to the Form hereafter following, or hath formerly had Episcopal Consecration, or Ordination.

9. Definition of Sacraments.[1]

Sacraments ordained of Christ be not only badges or tokens of men's professions, but rather they be certain sure witnesses, and effectual signs of grace, and God's goodwill towards us, by the which He doth work invisibly in us, and doth not only quicken but also strengthen and confirm our faith in Him.

10. The Two Sacraments.[2]

There are two Sacraments ordained of Christ our Lord in the Gospel, that is to say, Baptism and the Supper of the Lord.

---

[1] Article XXV.   [2] Ibid.

THE PRINCIPLES OF THE REFORMATION 31

11. *Repudiation of the Five Sacraments.*[1]

Those five commonly called Sacraments, that is to say, Confirmation, Penance, Orders, Matrimony, and Extreme Unction, are not to be accounted Sacraments of the Gospel, being such as have grown partly of the corrupt following of the Apostles, partly are states of life allowed in the Scriptures.

12. *Discouragement of non-communicating attendance.*[2]

The Sacraments were not ordained of Christ to be gazed upon, or to be carried about, but that we should duly use them.

13. *Definition of Baptismal Regeneration.*[3]

Baptism ... is also a sign of Regeneration, or new Birth, whereby, as by an instrument, they that receive Baptism rightly are grafted into the Church; the promises of forgiveness of sin, and of our adoption to be the sons of God by the Holy Ghost, are visibly signed and sealed; Faith is confirmed, and Grace increased by virtue of prayer unto God.

14. *Christ's Presence Spiritual.*[4]

The Body of Christ is given, taken, and eaten in the Supper, only after an heavenly and spiritual manner. And the mean whereby the Body of Christ is received and eaten in the Supper is Faith.

15. *Eucharistic Elevation and Worship forbidden.*[5]

The Sacrament of the Lord's Supper was not by Christ's ordinance reserved, carried about, lifted up, or worshipped.

16. *Warning against Superstition.*[6]

Whereas it is ordained in this office for the Administration of the Lord's Supper, that the Communicants should receive the same kneeling (which order is well meant, for a signification of our humble and grateful acknowledgment of the benefits of Christ therein given to all worthy Receivers, and for the avoiding

---

[1] Article XXV. [2] Ibid. [3] Article XXVII.
[4] Article XXVIII. [5] Ibid.
[6] Rubric at the end of the Communion Office.

of such profanation and disorder as might otherwise ensue); yet lest the same kneeling should by any persons, either out of ignorance or infirmity, or out of malice and obstinacy, be misconstrued and depraved; It is hereby declared, That thereby no adoration is intended, or ought to be done, either unto the Sacramental Bread or Wine there bodily received, or unto any Corporal Presence of Christ's natural Flesh and Blood. For the Sacramental Bread and Wine remain still in their very natural substances, and therefore may not be adored (for that were Idolatry, to be abhorred of all faithful Christians); and the natural Body and Blood of our Saviour Christ are in Heaven, and not here; it being against the truth of Christ's natural Body to be at one time in more places than one.

17. *The Cup for the Laity.*[1]

The Cup of the Lord is not to be denied to the Lay people; for both the parts of the Lord's Sacrament, by Christ's ordinance and commandment, ought to be ministered to all Christian men alike.

18. *Christ's Sacrifice complete for ever.*[2]

The Offering of Christ once made is that perfect redemption, propitiation, and satisfaction, for all the sins of the whole world, both original and actual; and there is none other satisfaction for sin, but that alone. Wherefore the sacrifices of Masses, in the which it was commonly said that the Priest did offer Christ for the quick and the dead, to have remission of pain or guilt, were blasphemous fables and dangerous deceits.

Who made there (by His one oblation of Himself once offered) a full, perfect, and sufficient sacrifice, oblation, and satisfaction for the sins of the whole world: and did institute, and in His holy Gospel command us to continue, a perpetual memory of that His precious death until His coming again.

19. *Object of the Lord's Supper.*[3]

Why was the Sacrament of the Lord's Supper ordained?—For the continual remembrance of the sacrifice of the death of Christ, and of the benefits which we receive thereby.

---

[1] Article XXX.   [2] Article XXXI.   [3] Catechism.

20. *No exhortation to fasting reception.*[1]

What is required of them who come to the Lord's Supper ?— To examine themselves, whether they repent them truly of their former sins; steadfastly purposing to lead a new life; have a lively faith in God's mercy through Christ, with a thankful remembrance of His death; and be in charity with all men.

21. *No change of ceremonies without special authority.*[2]

It is not necessary that Traditions and Ceremonies be in all places one, and utterly like; for at all times they have been divers, and may be changed according to the diversities of countries, times, and men's manners, so that nothing be ordained against God's Word. Whosoever through His private judgment, willingly and purposely, doth openly break the traditions and ceremonies of the Church, which be not repugnant to the Word of God, and be ordained and approved by common authority, ought to be rebuked openly (that others may fear to do the like), as he that offendeth against the common order of the Church, and hurteth the authority of the Magistrate, and woundeth the consciences of the weak brethren.

22. *Independence of National Churches in their ritual.*[3]

Every particular or National Church hath authority to ordain, change, and abolish ceremonies or rites of the Church ordained only by man's authority, so that all things be done to edifying.

23. *No ceremonies recognised except those in the Prayer-book.*[4]

The Book of Common Prayer and Administration of the Sacraments and other Rites and Ceremonies of the Church according to the use of the Church of England.

24. *The particular forms of Worship matters of indifference.*[5]

The particular forms of Divine Worship, and the Rites and Ceremonies to be used therein, being things in their own nature indifferent, and alterable, and so acknowledged; it is but reasonable that, upon weighty and important considerations, according

---

[1] Catechism.   [2] Article XXXIV.   [3] Ibid.
[4] Title-page of the Prayer-book.   [5] Preface to the Prayer-book.

to the exigency of times and occasions, such changes and alterations should be made therein, as to those that are in place of authority should from time to time seem necessary or expedient.

25. *Complexity to be avoided.*[1]

The godly and decent order of the ancient Fathers hath been altered, broken, and neglected . . . with multitude of Responds, Verses, vain repetitions, commemorations, and synodals.

26. *Uniformity desirable.*[2]

Whereas heretofore there hath been great diversity in saying and singing in Churches within this Realm; some following Salisbury use, some Hereford use, and some the use of Bangor, some of York, some of Lincoln; now from henceforth all the whole realm shall have but one use.

27. *The Bishop to decide in cases of doubt.*[3]

Forasmuch as nothing can be so plainly set forth, but doubts may arise in the use and practice of the same; to appease all such diversity (if any arise), and for the resolution of all doubts, concerning the manner how to understand, do, and execute, the things contained in this Book; the parties that so doubt, or diversely take anything, shall always resort to the Bishop of the Diocese, who by his discretion shall take order for the quieting and appeasing of the same; so that the same order be not contrary to anything contained in this Book. And if the Bishop of the Diocese be in doubt, then he may send for the resolution thereof to the Archbishop.

28. *Vow of obedience to the Bishop.*[4]

Will you reverently obey your Ordinary, and other chief Ministers, unto whom is committed the charge and government over you; following with a glad mind and will their godly admonitions, and submitting yourselves to their godly judgments?—I will so do, the Lord being my helper.

---

[1] "Concerning the Service of the Church."   [2] Ibid.
[3] Ibid.   [4] Ordination Service.

THE PRINCIPLES OF THE REFORMATION 35

29. *Pre-reformation Ceremonies unprofitable.*[1]

Of such Ceremonies as be used in the Church, and have had their beginning by the institution of man, some at the first were of godly intent and purpose devised, and yet at length turned to vanity and superstition; some entered into the Church by indiscreet devotion, and such a zeal as was without knowledge; and for because they were winked at in the beginning, they grew daily to more and more abuses, which not only for their unprofitableness, but also because they have much blinded the people, and obscured the glory of God, are worthy to be cut away and clean rejected.

30. *Wilful transgressing of a Common Order.*[2]

Although the keeping or omitting of a ceremony, in itself considered, is but a small thing; yet the wilful and contemptuous transgressing of a common order and discipline is of no small offence before God. "Let all things be done among you," saith St. Paul, "in a seemly and due order;" the appointment of the which order pertaineth not to private men; therefore no man ought to take in hand, nor presume to appoint or alter any public or common order in Christ's Church, except he be lawfully called and authorised thereunto.

31. *Christ's Gospel not a Ceremonial Law.*[3]

Some [Ceremonies] are put away, because the great excess and multitude of them hath so increased in these latter days, that the burden of them was intolerable; whereof St. Augustine in his time complained, that they were grown to such a number, that the estate of Christian people was in worse case concerning that matter, than were the Jews. And he counselled that such yoke and burden should be taken away, as time would serve quietly to do it. But what would St. Augustine have said if he had seen the Ceremonies of late days used among us: whereunto the multitude used in his time was not to be compared? This our excessive multitude of Ceremonies was so great, and many of them so dark, that they did more confound and darken than declare and set forth Christ's benefits unto us. And besides, Christ's Gospel is not a Ceremonial Law (as much of Moses' Law

---

[1] "Of Ceremonies."   [2] Ibid.   [3] Ibid.

was), but it is a religion to serve God, not in bondage of the figure or shadow, but in the freedom of the Spirit.

32. *The Royal Supremacy.*[1]

We give not to our Princes the ministering either of God's Word, or of the Sacraments . . . but that only prerogative, which we see to have been given always to all godly Princes in Holy Scripture by God Himself; that is, that they should rule all states and degrees committed to their charge by God, whether they be Ecclesiastical or Temporal, and restrain with the civil sword the stubborn and evil-doers.

33. *Independence of the Western Patriarchate.*[2]

The Bishop of Rome hath no jurisdiction in this Realm of England.

34. *Communion every Sunday not absolutely ordered except in Cathedral and Collegiate Churches and Colleges where there are many Priests and Deacons.*[3]

Upon the Sundays and other Holy-days (if there be no Communion) shall be said all that is appointed at the Communion until the end of the general Prayer for the whole state of Christ's Church militant here in earth, together with one or more of these Collects last before rehearsed, concluding with the Blessing.

In Cathedral and Collegiate Churches and Colleges, where there are many Priests and Deacons, they shall all receive the Communion with the Priest every Sunday at the least.

35. *Other Grace besides Sacramental.*[4]

They which be endued with so excellent a benefit of God be called according to God's purpose by His Spirit working in due season: they through Grace obey the calling: they be justified freely: they be made sons of God by adoption: they be made like the image of His only-begotten Son Jesus Christ: they walk religiously in good works, and at length, by God's mercy, they attain to everlasting felicity.

---

[1] Article XXXVII.   [2] Ibid.
[3] Rubrics at the end of the Communion Office.   [4] Article XVII.

These quotations are sufficient to sketch the general outline of English Reformation principles. Some of them would, of course, be acknowledged without modification by the new sacerdotal school; but the sacerdotal school no longer conceals its discontent with the Prayer-book as well as the Articles. It is because of the predominance of these principles that those who are represented by "the Lord's Day and the Holy Eucharist" wish to alter the Prayer-book. Their most sincere and sympathetic adherents amongst the clergy would probably be found now amongst those who subscribe to the great Evangelical societies. Amongst that large central mass of moderate clergymen who conform quietly to the prevailing tone of the time, who do not look very deeply into matters of controversy, and whose weight does not count very greatly in either direction, there would also be a very considerable number who, when the issue should be put to them clearly, would not wish the Reformation undone in such very serious matters as are now suggested. Amongst the old-fashioned High Churchmen—the men of the school of Hooker—there would also probably be many who prefer on the whole that things should remain as they are. The vast majority of laymen have not the least conception of the meaning of the tendency which is gradually being brought to bear upon them, nor of the proportions to which the sacerdotal movement has grown. They like beauty and solemnity in their services, but all their religious ideas are in the groove of the Reformation.

They joined instinctively some years ago in the short-sighted policy of Lord Beaconsfield's attempt to "put down Ritualism" by Act of Parliament, but they did not in the least measure the forces that were against them, nor see how strong was the grasp which the mediæval spirit had taken of a large and constantly increasing section of the clergy.

Some of the leading men of the Church would rather hear no more about the distinctive principles of the English Reformation. They are justly anxious for the peace and cohesion of the National Communion, and they consider that it should be maintained on the terms of those who have shown themselves to be most in downright earnest about propagating their opinions—the new sacerdotal school. Lord Halifax has some show of reason for speaking of "the Catholic Revival, which has transformed the Church of England, and is now thankfully accepted by the authorities of the Church."[1] And the adherents of the principles of the Reformation have made many disastrous blunders. They have, in the American phrase, "given themselves away." The policy, pursued by a section of them in appealing to the law—the policy, as it has appeared to the new sacerdotal school, of persecution—has alike, whether victorious or unsuccessful, given a greater stimulus than any other contrivance could have supplied to the distinctive pre-Reformation sentiment, opinions, and practices. The determination of many of them to

[1] "The Lord's Day and the Holy Eucharist," p. 26.

THE PRINCIPLES OF THE REFORMATION

adhere to a merely accidental type of ecclesiastical decoration, arrangement and musical rendering, and the refusal to accept the results in the national character and culture of that great wave of taste known as the Romantic Revival—introduced into this country by Sir Walter Scott, Southey, and Coleridge—have withdrawn from their support immense numbers of educated men and women. They have not realised the lesson of the fact that the true home of religious music and oratorio is evangelical Germany. Ninety-nine hundredths of those who think they prefer "High Church" to "Low Church" do so solely because they identify "High Church" with beauty, solemnity, and "hearty services," "Low Church" with ugliness and dulness. And again, the more conscious and strict adherents of Reformation principles have been lacking in leadership. That they have been marvellously abundant in good works is evidenced by the annual report and meeting of the Church Missionary Society, and by the subscription-lists of countless philanthropic enterpises; but they have not known how to make their influence felt in the affairs of the Church and nation at large. They have, to a great extent, stood aloof from Convocation, Church congresses, diocesan conferences. Their training colleges for a growing supply of young ministers have been few and far between. Though their general popular literature is enormous, they have absolutely no propaganda of the distinctive principles which give them their situation in the Church, the distinctive principles of the Reformation, as some would say with confidence—especially since the latest development of the pre-Reformation school—the distinctive principles of the Prayer-book. Young people, becoming alive to these things, and asking for Church principles, have been obliged to receive them from the literature which is more or less tinged with the new sacerdotal spirit. And the very simplicity of plain Primitive and Scriptural principles will always, as our Lord and St. Paul warned us, attract to itself a very large amount of intellectual scorn. There was something to be seen of this during the days of the Tractarian movement. It shows itself constantly in the writings of even the holiest and best men of that movement. The new school, on the other hand, has had every conceivable advantage: persecution, imprisonment, the ablest possible leaders, the most eloquent preachers, lives of conspicuous devotion, the support of the example of the mediæval churches in the East and West from the end of the third century to the present day, an unexpected amount of public patronage, a wide encouragement on the part of some of the Bishops —some on account of admiration for good works and lives, some on account of sympathy with principles— the general acceptance of the theory constantly repeated that when a diocese, cathedral or parish has once been won to the sacerdotal movement it must never again be conceded to distinctive Reformation principles, the hearty adoption by the movement of the simultaneous impulse in favour of Romantic forms in architecture, music and taste, a perseverance and cohesion amongst themselves which the other side have been unable to show, a skill and ability worthy of their great leader Newman himself (of whom we are told that he almost made the Church of England as we see it), and of the famous Tract XC.

Would it not be better to accept the policy of deliberate silence, join heartily with the sacerdotal movement, drop whatever is distinctly non-sacerdotal about the Reformation, never mention its principles in public teaching, and leave them entirely to the Nonconformists?

It is absolutely and fundamentally impossible. Adherence to the principles of the English Reformation is no mere *esprit de corps* or family tradition. It is with those who understand and hold them a matter of vital truth; with them the Scriptures will always be the supreme authority in faith. The men who handed down the Scriptures did not invent the words which give them their sole importance. Their sole importance lies in the fact that they contain the living words of the Son of God, the inspired words of inspired Apostles. Among witnesses to Holy Scripture and its meaning the Primitive Church is pre-eminent in importance, but at no time has the Church been infallible. The word "Catholic" has a spurious use when it is applied to any possible developments or institutions of a Church calling itself Catholic. Its true use was defined by

St. Vincent of Lérins: "Quod semper, quod ubique, quod ab omnibus." That must include the most important time of all, the time of the New Testament itself. The episcopal form of government is true in fact and fitness; but there is nothing in Scripture to suggest the doctrinal theories of a mystic Apostolical succession. The Christian minister is a Presbyter, not technically a Sacerdos.[1] Baptismal regeneration is a new birth into conditions of spiritual influence. There are many means of grace, of which Holy Communion holds an important place. The minister is not technically, but only metaphorically, a sacrificer; for the sacrifice which is commemorated was Christ's death upon the cross for our redemption, Who made there, by His one oblation of Himself once offered, a full, perfect, and sufficient sacrifice, oblation, and satisfaction for the sins of the whole world, and did institute, and in His holy Gospel command us to continue, a perpetual memory (in no sense a revival) of that His precious death until His coming again.[2] What we offer to God at the Holy Communion is money, unconsecrated bread, unconsecrated wine, oblations in kind, as symbols of His gifts, and prayers: "We humbly beseech Thee most mercifully to accept our alms and oblations, and to receive these our prayers, which we offer unto Thy

---

[1] Bishop Lightfoot, *Epistle to the Philippians*, "Christian Ministry," p. 191.
[2] Waterland, "Doctrine of the Eucharist," chap. xii. p. 313 (1880); Hooker, *Eccl. Pol.* Book V. chap. lxvii. 12.

THE PRINCIPLES OF THE REFORMATION 43

Divine Majesty;"[1] we offer gratitude: " We, Thy humble servants, entirely desire Thy Fatherly goodness mercifully to accept this our sacrifice of praise and thanksgiving;"[2] and we offer ourselves: " Here we offer and present unto Thee, O Lord, ourselves, our souls and bodies, to be a reasonable, holy, and lively sacrifice unto Thee. . . . And though we be unworthy through our manifold sins to offer unto Thee any sacrifice, yet we beseech Thee to accept this our bounden duty and service; not weighing our merits, but pardoning our offences." To the adherent of Reformation principles the service is rightly called " The administration of the Lord's Supper," and the Board " The Lord's Table." The presence of our Lord is spiritual; the body of Christ is given, taken, and eaten only after a heavenly and spiritual manner; and the means whereby the body of Christ is received and eaten in the Supper is faith. The adherents of English Reformation principles believe that all rites, ceremonies, and doctrines outside the Prayer-book were, according to the title and prefaces, deliberately dismissed at the time of the Reformation, and they are content that it should be so. They believe that, as to ecclesiastical dress, the custom of three hundred years is a sufficient guide; they wish to wear what will as little as possible call away attention from weightier things, so long as decency and order are observed, in accordance with primitive principle. They

[1] Prayer for the Church Militant.
[2] Concluding Prayer.

find that in the Primitive Church, as well as at the Reformation, the laity had a due share with the clergy in the settlement of the affairs of the Church, and they are opposed to exclusive clerical domination. They accept equally the civil and ecclesiastical jurisdiction, each in its own sphere. They altogether distrust tradition, remembering that a false tradition about the meaning of our Lord's parting words to St. Peter about St. John was current even amongst the Apostles themselves.[1] They adhere to the principle of National Churches as an obviously convenient and natural arrangement, dating from the time when the Roman Empire broke up into the Teutonic kingdoms, and they are jealous of the members of one National Church borrowing the principles and customs of another without due authority.

These are, to speak quite generally, some of the distinctive principles and ideas of the Reformation as over against the principles and ideas of the previous era. Perhaps an official who, from his position, is obliged to stand outside all party combinations, is in a better situation to estimate fairly the prospects of these principles and ideas than any who are members of particular sacerdotal or Evangelical organisations.

First, these principles will assuredly never die. They appear to be founded alike in history and Scripture, and they have been the strongest moral force the country has ever known. Fortunately, the intercourse between the two sides of the National Church is frequent and

[1] St. John xxi. 23.

friendly, and many who believe themselves to be rigidly and exclusively sacerdotal are, in reality, largely under the influence of Reformation ideas. In the general consent of the present age to abandon all authority and discipline, except in matters of morality, such a mixture of ideas is a very probable result. The important thing is that those on whom these principles depend for their maintenance should understand in what way they are essential to their position.

Secondly, the position of those who accept the English Reformation is immensely strong in the fact that the formularies of the Church of England were arranged by those who carried out the Reformation, and as a plain matter of fact express their convictions. They are, as yet, intact and unchanged. And any serious demand for change on the part of the new sacerdotal school would be in the last degree unwise from their own point of view; the laity would probably insist on, at least, an equal share in such a revision with that which they had at the time of the Reformation, and it is quite possible, when it should come to an actual matter of practical fact instead of talk, that the sacerdotal school might lose more than it had hoped to gain. An absurd mistake has been made, both by secular journals and by simple and unthinking clergymen, when they have noticed the advice of some of the Bishops to their dioceses to accept the Lincoln Judgment. It has been supposed that all who did not before use the disputed practices were now to adopt them.

What the Bishops meant was obviously that none were to do the things that had been forbidden. All that has been decided is that such practices are not inconsistent with a conceivable interpretation of the law. Those who did not use them are left entirely where they were.

Thirdly, the adherents of the principles of the Reformation have the laity behind them. There can be no doubt of that. The laity do not know much of mediæval doctrines, and perhaps less of controversy; but they understand and love the Bible, and they have an undying and inextinguishable hatred of priestcraft. That is enough. Where the extreme churches have attracted large numbers of men, it has been, in my experience, through the commanding personality and supreme earnestness of individual preachers. In the main, like the system of the great Roman Church, the movement has depended more on the emotions of devout women than on the intelligence of men. Scepticism, throughout the course of history, has attended as a Nemesis on distorted and disproportionate religious belief.

Fourthly, a great access of strength will necessarily come to the adherents of Reformation principles now that they have dropped the fatal policy of persecution, or prosecution, let it be called what it may. All talk about forming a Parliamentary party and obtaining legislative changes is futile. It can only increase the cohesion of those against whom the weapon is directed, and react unfavourably on the condition and estimation of those who employ it. Spiritual matters must be dealt with spiritually, that is, by discussion, arguments, appeals to Scripture and the Primitive Church, by love and by prayer.

Fifthly, the friends of the Reformation, it is plain, will now direct their energies to legitimate missionary efforts at home. They will study more deeply the history of the principles which they profess, explain them in clear and simple language, and bring them within reach of every home in the country. The vast sums which they have spent on litigation will now be free for the education of young men for the ministry, and the erection of theological colleges and middle-class schools. Having learnt the lesson that bitterness and invective only recoil on those who indulge in them, all their efforts will be animated by the Christian graces of candour, humility, and patience.

III.

THE POSITION OF THE LAITY IN THE PRIMITIVE CHURCH

"I would demand what evidence there is, which way it may clearly be showed, that in ancient kingdoms Christian, any canon devised by the clergy alone in their synods, whether provincial, national, or general, hath by mere force of their agreement taken place as a law, making all men constrainable to be obedient thereunto."—HOOKER.[1]

IN the New Testament we do not need reminding that all Christians alike were termed in a spiritual sense priests, in regard to their holiness and privileges. It is no less certain that in every congregation men were appointed to be rulers. The authority was of two kinds—that of the Word preached, and that of the office-bearer within his own sphere. Obedience to the first was absolute, so far as the preaching was true to the Word. The second kind of authority was limited and liable to modification, inasmuch as it was representative of the whole body of the "Church," by whom these office-bearers were elected, with the addition of the sanction of the superior office-bearers already existing. I would refer to such well-known passages as Heb. xiii.

---

[1] *Eccl. Pol.* VIII. vi. 9.

17; 1 Thess. v. 12; 1 Tim. iii. 5; v. 17; 1 Tim. iv. 6, 11.¹

The laity, however, who were called in the New Testament "The Brethren," retained co-ordinate rights of their own. When Paul and Barnabas came to Jerusalem it was not merely the apostles and elders who formally received them, but the whole Church. When an official letter is sent to the Gentiles it is not merely by the apostles and elders, but by the whole Church. And the letter was sent "to the brethren" alone; to the brethren alone it contained greeting. The letter itself was delivered, not to the rulers of the Church at Antioch, but to the whole multitude.²

Again: the precedent was undoubtedly followed by which laymen duly qualified might give instruction among the Jews. In the synagogues, says Mr. Scudamore in the Dictionary of Christian Antiquities,³ it was usual for the elder to ask any one of repute to comment on the lesson for the day (Luke iv. 17; Acts xvii. 2), or to deliver a word of exhortation (Acts xiii. 15). This liberty was certainly continued under the gospel in the case of those who had either the gift of prophecy, or of tongues, or of interpretation (Rom. xii. 6; 1 Cor. xii. 10, 28; xiv. 1–6, 31, &c.). St. Paul's rubric is perfectly plain: "When ye come together, every one

---

[1] Compare Moberley's Bampton Lectures, p. 117, and note W.

[2] Compare the evidence of the Didachè, and the illustrations of the jurisdiction of the "Church" over its clergy in the Epistle of St. Clement.

[3] *Dictionary of Christian Antiquities*, Article "Laity."

of you hath a psalm, hath a doctrine, hath a tongue, hath a revelation, hath an interpretation. Let all things be done unto edifying. If any man speak in an unknown tongue let it be by two, or at the most by three, and that by course; and let one interpret. But if there be no interpreter let him keep silence in the Church; and let him speak to himself and to God. Let the prophets speak two or three, and let the other judge. If anything be revealed to another that sitteth by, let the first hold his peace. For ye may all prophecy one by one, that all may learn, and all may be comforted."[1]

Among unbelievers, continues Mr. Scudamore, all Christians were expected to teach the gospel as opportunity was given. They that were scattered abroad by the persecution on the death of Stephen went everywhere preaching the Word (Acts viii. 4). The majority of these would be laymen. Thus St. Paul, before he received the laying on of hands, preached boldly at Damascus in the name of Jesus (Acts xiii. 3 ; ix. 27); Aquila and Priscilla expounded unto Apollos the way of God more perfectly (Acts xviii. 26); and Apollos himself mightily convinced the Jews, and that publicly, shewing by the Scriptures that Jesus was Christ (Acts xviii. 28). Hilary the Deacon informs us that "At first all taught and baptized on whatever days and seasons occasion required. . . . That the people might grow and multiply, it was at the beginning permitted to all

[1] 1 Cor. xiv. 26.

to preach the gospel, and to baptize, and to explain the Scriptures in church; but when the Church embraced all places, houses of assembly were constituted, and rulers (rectors), and other offices in the Church were constituted. . . . Hence it is that now neither do deacons preach in the congregation, nor clerks nor laymen baptize" (Hilar. Diac. *Comm. in Ep. ad Eph.* iv. 11, 12.[1]

An illustrious example of this right of the laity is seen in the case of Justin Martyr. Clothed in the philosopher's cloak, which gave him a title to be heard in public places, Justin devoted his life to the support of his new faith as an itinerant evangelist, with no office in the Church. His calling is expressed in his own words: "Every one who can preach the truth, and does not preach it, incurs the judgment of God." It was the same with most of the other Apologists. The office of Catechist has also an important bearing on the subject.

Even inside the Church, in the most settled times alluded to by Hilary the Deacon, lay preaching was encouraged. When Demetrius, Bishop of Alexandria, complained that Origen, who was not a priest, had been asked by the Bishops of the district to interpret Holy Scripture publicly in church at Cæsarea, the Bishops of Jerusalem and Cæsarea denied the validity of one

---

[1] Hilary's words are very remarkable: "Et cœpit *alio* ordine et providentia gubernari ecclesia;" "and the Church began to be governed by *another* order and plan."

ground taken by Bishop Demetrius, namely, that laymen had never been known to preach before Bishops. "If," said they, "any persons are anywhere found capable of benefiting the brethren, they are encouraged by the holy Bishops to preach to the people. Thus at Larandi, Euelpis was asked by Neon; and at Iconium, Paulinus by Celsus; and at Smyrna, Theodore by Atticus;—our brethren now in bliss. And it is probable that this thing has been done in other places without our knowing it" (Euseb. *Hist. Eccl.* vi. 19). Frumentius and Ædesius, while laymen, laid the foundation of the Church in Abyssinia (Socr. *Hist. Eccl.* i. 19). The same service was rendered to Iberia (Georgia) by a female captive, who having healed by her prayers the king and his wife and son, exhorted them to believe in Christ, through whose Name their cure had been effected (ib. c. 20).[1]

Even as late as A.D. 398 a Council held at Carthage was content with forbidding a layman to teach in the presence of clerics unless they themselves asked him. It was not till 453 that Leo I., writing to Maximus, Patriarch of Antioch, in view of the danger arising

---

[1] The restrictions placed on laymen, and varied from time to time, were rather matters of Church order, to avoid schisms and scandals, than of necessary principles. In the same way there are synodical decrees forbidding presbyters to baptize or celebrate in the presence of the Bishop, or without his license; *e.g.*, the Second Council of Seville, A.D 619. Even Ignatius tells the Philadelphians that their bishop "had obtained the ministry *which pertaineth to all in common.*" Compare Manley's Hulsean Lecture on the Presbyterate, pp. 2, note, and 56.

from the growth of the Nestorian and Eutychian heresies, with all their intricacies and subtleties, entreats him to take order that beside those who are presbyters of the Lord, no one presume to claim for himself the right to teach or to preach, whether he be monk or layman (Epist. 92, c. 6). It was not till A.D. 691 that the Council *in Trullo*, at Constantinople, declares " that a layman ought not to dispute or teach publicly, thence arrogating to himself the right to teach." With such late decisions in a corrupt age we have no concern whatever.

We now pass to baptism by laymen. In the fourth century there seems to have been an opinion that laymen could not baptize. It was held by the Greek compiler of the Clementine Constitutions, and perhaps by St. Basil.

The evidence on the other side is strong. Tertullian, whom St. Cyprian used to call his master, teaches that abstractedly laymen have power to baptize, but that they can only exercise it by permission, expressed or understood.[1] He argues that what is received equally by all can be imparted equally by all; but he adds, How much more is the discipline of reverence and modesty incumbent on the laity, seeing that it is the part of those greater than themselves, *i.e.*, the presbyters, not to take on themselves the episcopate, which is assigned to the Bishops.[2] Emulation is the mother of schisms (de Baptiz. 17).

[1] The same permission was required by presbyter and deacon.
[2] The fact that the Bishop's authority is *delegated* to him by the

There is a story told by Rufinus, A.D. 390 (*Hist. Eccl.* i. 14), of some boys baptized in play by Athanasius when himself quite a child (Socr. A.D. 439, *Hist. Eccl.* i. 15). The Bishop of Alexandria, who happened to see what was done from a distance, finding on inquiry that water had been duly used, and the right form of words said, decided, after conference with his clergy, that the children should not be rebaptized, but he supplemented their irregular baptism by confirming them himself. The story would not have been related by Rufinus, or repeated at length by Sozomen, A.D. 460 (*Hist. Eccl.* ii. 17), without some protest if the ground on which the Bishop acted had not been widely accepted in the Church at the time.

It is from the Council of Elvira, about A.D. 300, that we first learn under what circumstances it was held lawful for a layman to baptize. The 38th Canon decrees that "during foreign travel, at sea, or if there be no church near, one of the faithful, who has his own baptism entire (*i.e.*, not clinic, duly confirmed, and not vitiated by lapse), and is not a bigamist, may baptize a catechumen in extremity of sickness, on condition that if he recover he take him to the Bishop to receive the benefit of the laying on of hands." St. Jerome, writing in 378, says, "Baptism we know to be often

---

people is strongly insisted upon by Alcuin. Churton, in his preface to Pearson's works, quotes Alcuin as saying: "Non omnis presbyter episcopus, quia ad unum omnis sollicitudo ecclesiæ quasi ad patrem *delegata* est, qui quasi filios diligat et gubernat, non tribunitiâ potestate sed pietate paternâ."

permitted to laymen, if necessity compel. For as one receives, so can he also give." St. Augustine, about 400, says: "If any layman, compelled by necessity, shall have given to a dying man that which when he received it himself he learnt the manner of giving, I know not if any man could piously say that it ought to be repeated. For to do it without necessity is to usurp the office of another; but to do it under pressure of necessity is either no fault or a venial." Shortly after this he shows a disposition to go farther, and to recognise the outward act under whatever circumstances performed. He is speaking of several questions which might be raised; baptism by one unbaptized; whether it is valid, whatever the faith, motive, or position of the giver and receiver? He even includes baptism on the stage where the actors are heathens, leaning to the affirmative if the recipient receives a sudden access of faith. He would in all such questions defer to a plenary council; an answer to the last must be sought by most earnest and united prayer. He adds that, at all events, he would at such a council not hesitate to maintain that they have baptism who have received it consecrated by the words of the Gospel, anywhere and from any one whomsoever without deceit on their part, and with some faith.

In a passage in a letter in question ascribed to St. Augustine there is a story, which the writer admits to be uncertain, of a catechumen and a penitent in danger of being shipwrecked together. As they were the only Christians in the ship, the penitent baptized the catechumen, and was in turn reconciled by him. What they did was approved.

With regard to the administration of Holy Communion, the position is different. There can be little doubt that in the earliest days of the Church, after our Lord's ascension, the Christians assembled daily in the houses each of the other and solemnly broke bread at the principal meal of the day, in strict obedience to our Lord's command.[1] It is equally clear that in the Church of Corinth, at any rate, this liberty was turned into licence, and led gradually to the separation of the breaking of bread from the united meal, and so to the service at which the Elder henceforth presided.[2]

I pass to another point. The election of ministers was either made directly by the people, or approved by them if the designation were made by the Bishop or the clergy. The consent of the whole congregation was required from the almost apostolic age of Clement of Rome (*Epist.* I ad. Cor. 44) down to and beyond the development of clerical authority in the days of Cyprian, who calls this "an apostolic and almost universal regulation" (*Epist.* ix. 3, 4). In the election of a Bishop the "*suffragium*" of the people accompanied

---

[1] Acts ii. 46.
[2] 1 Cor. xi. 20, 22, 33, 34. Compare also Dale's "Historical Essay," p. 52. The Elder presided when the gathering for breaking of bread ceased to be purely domestic. The meeting at Corinth was clearly public.

and often preceded the "judicium" of the clergy of the diocese; and elections by a spontaneous outburst of the popular voice were held valid in the cases of Cyprian, and afterwards of Athanasius and Ambrose. The rite of ordination was of course necessary for all grades of the ministry.[1]

The Council of Carthage in a Synodal Epistle declares that the nominations to all orders in the ministry must take place in presence of the people, before the eyes of all, and not without the knowledge of the bystanding multitude, so that the crimes of the wicked may be detected, and the virtues of the good declared.[2]

Laymen bore an important share in the General Councils. The Christian Emperors considered themselves entitled to select certain learned and distinguished laymen, conversant with ecclesiastical law and Christian doctrine, to sit in General Councils as members or assessors. These laymen bore the high title of Judices Gloriosissimi, and exercised a powerful and salutary influence over the assemblies in which they sat. In the proceedings of the Council of Chalcedon, the Judices Gloriosissimi are described as interposing an interlocution to this effect: *Videtur nobis justum esse, si placuerit Divinissime et piissime Domino nostro,* &c. Upon this follows their decree;

[1] The rite of ordination, Cheirothesia, was as it were the coronation, while the election, Cheirotonia, was the delegation to the office of the cleric.
[2] Charges of Archdeacon (John) Sinclair, p. 382; *cf.* also Conc Chalced., A.D. 451, Act xi.; Labbe, iv. 698.

and the Oriental Bishops, so far from considering them to have exceeded their prerogatives, exclaim, *Hoc justum judicium.* On another occasion the *Judices* require certain acts, which had been passed in their absence, to be read over, and afterwards inform the Council that they have submitted those acts to the Emperor, adding "*Expectamus pietatis ejus mandata.*"

One more point should be noticed, and that is the origin of lay patronage. The appointment of local clergy had very early fallen into the hands of the Bishops, though still with the assent, real or supposed, of the congregation. The Council of Orange, A.D. 441,[1] first extended episcopal patronage beyond a Bishop's own diocese, in the case of churches that he might have built in another; and a century later the Emperor Justinian, probably sanctioning a growing practice, granted the same privilege to laymen. His law of 541 enacted that any one who should found a church, and should endow it with maintenance for a clerk, might nominate a person who should be ordained to it. The Bishops were at liberty in such cases to refuse ordination if the individual presented were unfit.

In an epistle of Theodosius and Valentinian, the nave of the Church is called εὐκτήριον τοῦ λαοῦ. In a law of Justinian, A.D. 528, the clergy are exhorted to a punctual observance of their hours of prayer, by

---

[1] Landon's Manual of Councils, ii. 2. Compare Gall's *Synagogue* (Simpkin, Marshall, & Co.).

POSITION OF LAITY IN PRIMITIVE CHURCH 59

an appeal to the example of many of the laity, who for the good of their souls constantly frequent the very holy churches, and show themselves diligent in the practice of psalmody. From this Mr. Scudamore infers as probable that at that time laymen often met together in church to sing psalms out of the hours of public worship, and when the clergy were not present.

We have now seen that in the beginning the laity were on an equality with the clergy, submitting to the superintendence of the ruler whom they have themselves chosen, and who has been ordained by authority. We have seen them preaching without limitation out of doors, and with the consent of Bishop or clergy in the church. They baptize at first freely, afterwards in cases of necessity. They elect clergy [1] and Bishops.[2] At first in the very simplest days they break bread from house to house, but they soon lose this privilege through disorder. They receive letters from Apostles and Churches. They are represented by Imperial Commissioners in General Councils. They at last acquire the right to appoint to churches which they have built. At the present day, when Christian ministrations are

---

[1] This is now very feebly represented by the reading of the "Si quis" before ordination, to give opportunity for valid objection.

[2] This is represented by the nomination of a new Bishop to the Crown, as embodying the whole state, by the Prime Minister, who is himself practically the choice of the representatives of the people.

needed so sorely on all hands, we may well take these facts into our most serious consideration.[1]

[1] The Bishop of London has already appointed laymen to preach in churches at times other than those of the regular services. In the dearth of spiritual ministrations amongst the vast masses of our population, perhaps other opportunities may be discovered for lay work, under proper restrictions, in accordance with primitive precedent.

IV.

THE USE AND MEANING OF THE WORD CATHOLIC.

"Those who feel they can with a safe conscience remain with us while they are allowed to testify in behalf of '*Catholicism*,' and to promote its interests, *i.e.*, as if by such acts they were putting our Church, or at least a portion of it, in which they are included, in the position of catechumens. They think they may stay while they are moving themselves and others, nay, say the whole Church, towards Rome."—J. H. NEWMAN.[1]

IT is always difficult when you are close to a thing, and have been familiar with it for a very long time, to survey and measure it in its true proportions. And as the Church of Rome did for some 800 years bear a practically undisputed sway as the seat of the Patriarchate of the West, over Western Christendom, and as even since the disruption of the Reformation that Church has had by far the largest number of European Christians adhering to her allegiance, there has been a disposition on the part of a considerable number of very well-meaning persons in the English Church to take the customs and practices of the Church of Rome during the last 1200 years as a very fair witness of

[1] Life of Ward, Letter of Sept. 1843.

what ought rightly to be considered Catholic. The argument was, in defiance of St. Vincent of Lérins, that the dress, ritual, ceremonies, customs, and laws of a Church calling itself Catholic, must necessarily themselves be Catholic. I shall show presently that this is not the case according to true Catholic principles, but that the right to this authoritative title must in each particular case be investigated on its own merits. Many of these customs and practices go back to earlier times before the Church of Rome assumed so decided a lead, and the fact that they are to be found at a remote date seems to satisfy many devout minds that they must therefore be Catholic and worthy not merely of attention, but of deference, and even obedience.

It is, therefore, very desirable that we should examine this word Catholic, and settle for ourselves something of its history and of the limits of its jurisdiction. We cannot very well leave the delimitation of the sphere of such an important term to the vague piety and uninstructed enthusiasm of unauthorised persons, however admirable. It was first of all used in its ordinary sense of universal, not only by heathen authors such as Pliny, but also not uncommonly by ecclesiastical writers. Justin Martyr[1] speaks of the καθολίκη ἀνάστασις, meaning the general resurrection; Tertullian[2] talks of the *Catholica bonitas Dei*, the universal goodness of God. Then it came to be used as an epithet

[1] Dial. cum. Tryph. 81.   [2] Adv. Marcion. ii. 17.

MEANING OF THE WORD CATHOLIC

of the general Christian Church, faith, tradition, and people; among the first writers employing it being "Ignatius"[1] and Clement of Alexandria.[2] Then it was employed in the Creed of the Eastern Church, with reference to the whole body of Christians. This usage did not at first extend to the Western Church. It was employed in this significance also in the Creed of Arius. Next, it meant that portion of the Universal Church which was present in any particular place; probably as opposed to heretical bodies.[3] From this it was employed to mean Christian as constrasted with heathen, or orthodox as distinct from schismatics. Prudentius[4] speaks of *Catholica Fides, Catholici Populi;* Pacian[5] says, "*Christianus mihi nomen est, Catholicus cognomen.*" In the Council of Antioch in 341 A.D., *αἱ καθολίκαι ἐκκλησίαι* are spoken of in contrast to the followers of Paul of Samosata. In the Council of Rimini, in 359 A.D., *ἡ καθολίκη ἐκκλησία* occurs in opposition to heretics. So, in the Athanasian Creed, we have the Catholic Religion, the Catholic Faith. Later on, men were driven to find a *rationale* for the epithet, especially in the times of the Donatist controversy, when the Donatists said that it did not imply the communion of the whole world, but the keeping of all the Divine

---

[1] Ad. Smyrn. viii. [2] Strom. vii. p. 899, Oxf. 1715.
[3] It was the narrow sectarianism of the heretics as well as their errors that made them unworthy the name Catholic, *e.g.*, the Donatists. [4] *Peristeph.* iv. 24.
[5] Epist. 1, ad. Sempron.

commandments and sacraments. St. Augustine[1] accordingly takes it of the universality of the Church; so also Isidorus.[2] St. Cyril of Jerusalem[3] dilates on the word in this sense, as intimating that the Church subjugates all men, teaches all truth, heals all sin. In somewhat like way the General Epistles were in the third century called Catholic, because they were written to all. So at last we get to St. Vincent of Lérins, a well-known presbyter of Gaul who died about 450 A.D. He defined Catholic to mean, "*quod semper, quod ubique, quod ab omnibus*"—that which has been held always, everywhere, and by all alike. St. Vincent's definition has no specially binding authority of its own; but it has been generally accepted, and it appears true, both historically and theoretically. We need hardly seek for a better definition.[4]

Let us take three great authorities of our own Church, and see what they say about the use of the word in our creed. I do not know any English writers more serious, thoughtful, and authoritative than Bishop Pearson, Dean Field, and Dean Jackson. Pearson[5] takes up four points as implied by this important term: First, the diffusiveness of the Church, in fulfilment of the word, "Go, teach all nations;" second, the teaching of all things that are necessary for a Christian to know—

---

[1] Epist. 52, § i.   [2] Sentent. i. 16.   [3] Lect. Catech. xviii. § 23.

[4] Vincent uses it of doctrines; if the word is to have any meaning, it must of course be applied to customs and practices in the same way.

[5] Pearson "On the Creed," Art. IX.

this is probably derived from the language of St. Cyril of Jerusalem; third, the universal obedience amongst men of all conditions in performing the evangelical commands; fourth, the fact that all graces are given in it, whereby all the diseases of the soul are healed, spiritual virtues are disseminated, all the thoughts of men regulated, till we become perfect men in Christ Jesus. Pearson describes all true Churches added on to the Church which first began at Jerusalem as members of the Catholic Church. We may add that even Churches which have no visible intercommunion with other Churches by defect of government, as the Norwegian, Lutheran, and French Reformed Churches, or by necessary revolt, as our own English Church, do not assert that they are new Churches, but all alike claim to be considered branches of that which was begun at Jerusalem. In the same sense Dean Field writes:[1]—

"The title of Catholic doth most fitly express those, both Christian men and societies of Christians, who hold the common faith without division from the main body of Christianity. While, therefore, there was but the main body of Christianity at union within itself, and such portions of reduced and misled people as apparently divided themselves from it, the name of a Catholic was a note and distinctive mark or character to know and discern a Catholic from a heretic or schismatic by, and the naming after the name of any man a note of particularity, and heretical or schismatical

[1] Field, "On the Church," bk. ii. chap. ix.

faction. Whereupon one of the ancients said fitly to this purpose, 'Christian is my name and Catholic is my surname; by the one I am known from infidels, by the other from heretics and schismatics.' But when the main body of the Christian Church divided itself, partly by reason of different ceremonies, uses, customs, and observations; partly through the ambitious strivings of the Bishops and Prelates of the greatest, richest, and most respected places; partly by occasion of some different opinions; the name of Catholic remained common to either of the parts thus divided, sundered, and rent one from another, though on the one side rested not only error, but heresy also in the opinion of the other. With regard to the arbitrary assumption that the use of particular names was a sign of heresy, he points out that this would condemn those Churches which were called Ambrosian and those that were named by distinction Gregorian."

Dean Jackson,[1] in the same manner as Dean Field, sets aside the name Catholic as an inseparable mark of a true visible Church, on the ground of the divisions of Christendom. He shows that as there is a Catholic faith, so we of the Reformed Churches deserve the appellation far more truly than the Roman Church, because we have kept the Catholic Faith pure and undefiled, whereas they of the Roman Church have defiled and polluted it for many generations, and do still defile it, with many loathsome additions.

[1] Jackson's "Works," bk. xii. chap. xxii.

We have seen in the primitive use of the word how there was a Catholic Faith and a Catholic Church; I shall show how the modern use of the word as applied to ceremonies is altogether illogical. It is not difficult to establish what is the Catholic Faith. According to the accepted definition of Vincentius of Lérins, it must be that which has been held always, everywhere, and by everybody. The title Catholic will apply primarily to the Holy Scriptures, as they were gradually accepted by the whole Church, except the obvious and notorious heretics. It will apply in an almost equal degree to the Apostles' Creed, because none will seriously deny that this short summary of faith is overwhelmingly warranted by Holy Scripture. It will apply in a less degree, but still in a degree that is very strong, to the Nicene Creed. It is true that the Filioque clause has divided the East from the West, but still the main parts of the Nicene Creed are thoroughly universal in authority and acceptance. Beyond these two great Creeds, every Church has, of course, the right to adopt particular confessions of faith which suit the particular circumstances of each, and to claim that the phraseology of such additional confessions is in accordance with the ancient principles of universal truth; but such confessions, however useful and necessary, cannot be, in the true sense of the word, catholic and universal, because, plainly, both in their origin and in their use they are particular. The Athanasian Creed teaches important Catholic doctrine, but it cannot itself claim the title of a Catholic document, as it was never universally received, and was originally special to the Church of France. (Gaul)

Nor is it very difficult to ascertain what is meant by the Catholic Church. Let us go again to Dean Field.

"The special points (he says) which we are, in the Article of the Holy Catholic Church, to believe, are these: First, that as Christ while He lived on earth was a King, albeit His kingdom was not earthly nor of this world, so He hath still a kingdom or at least a great part of His kingdom, here on earth, the members or citizens of which kingdom, whilst living in this world, are not of this world; their πολίτευμα (as our Apostle speaks) is in heaven; that is, the society or corporation whereof they are actual and live members is translated from earth to heaven. . . . The second, that God or Christ, in the choice or admission of citizens into this celestial corporation, doth not tie Himself to any one kingdom, nation, or province, to any visible society or corporation here on earth. But as heaven itself is alike distant from every part of the earth, so every nation or kingdom of the earth are alike free to stand for, or solicit their election or admission into, this heavenly society which we term the Holy Catholic Church. Of these two branches of belief this third is a necessary consequent, that God hath not bestowed such privileges upon any visible church or ecclesiastical society whatsoever upon the

really? Truth is that Christ founded

face of the whole earth, as divers founders of colleges in our universities have done upon some grammar schools likewise founded by them. Many have been chosen and admitted for perpetual fellows of the celestial academy, which were never trained up in the doctrine or discipline of the Grecian, English, or Roman Church. God is the sole founder of the universal Church, and of every particular true Church. As for particular visible churches, all are alike free, all their sons alike capable of admission into the Holy Catholic Church; or if any odds there be, it is in the different measure of their observance of the laws prescribed to all, especially the law of loving God above all in Christ, and of loving others as ourselves for Christ's sake."

On this subject of the word Catholic as applied to the Church, I will refer once more to Dean Field. In the Second Book, chapter 2, he gives three "proper and peculiar notes," which absolutely "distinguish the true Catholic Church":—

"I. The entire profession of those supernatural verities which God hath revealed in Christ His Son.

"II. The use of such holy ceremonies and sacraments as He hath instituted and appointed to serve as provocations to godliness, preservations from sin, memorials of the benefits of Christ, warrants for the greater security of our belief, and marks of distinction to separate His own from strangers.

"III. A union or connection of men in this profession and use of these sacraments, under lawful pastors and guides, appointed, authorised, and sanctified, to direct and lead them in the happy ways of eternal salvation."

In the 5th chapter of the Second Book, Field discusses the five notes of the Church given by Cardinal Bellarmine :—

"I. Antiquity.
"II. Succession.
"III. Unity.
"IV. Universality.
"V. The very name and title of Catholic expressing the universality."

He shows the uncertainty of these points, explains in what sense they are important, and demonstrates their failure as true notes of the Church.

Bishop Pearson, in discussing the Article of the Creed, "The Holy Catholic Church," or "I believe in one Holy Catholic Church," after exemplifying the plural use of the word in the New Testament, speaks as follows :—

"Now as several churches are reduced to the denomination of one Church in relation to the single governor of those many churches, so all the churches of all cities and all nations in the world may be reduced to the same single denomination in relation to one Supreme Governor of them all, and that one Governor is Christ, the Bishop of our souls. Wherefore, the Apostle, speaking of that in which all churches do agree, comprehendeth them all under the same appellation of one Church; and, therefore, often by the name of Church are understood all Christians whatsoever belonging to any of the churches dispersed throughout the distant and divided parts of the world. For the single persons professing faith in Christ are members of the particular churches in which they live, and all those particular churches are members of the general and universal Church, which is one by unity of aggregation; and this is the Church in the creed we believe, and which is in other creeds expressly termed one: I believe in one Holy Catholic Church. It will, therefore, be further necessary for the understanding of the nature of the Church which is thus one, to consider in what that unity doth consist. And being as it is an aggregation not only of many persons, but also of many congregations, the unity thereof must consist in some agreement of them all, and adhesion to something which is one. If, then, we reflect upon the first Church again, which we found constituted in the Acts, and to which all others since have been in a manner added and conjoined, we may collect from their doctrine and agreement how all other Churches are united and agree. Now, they were described to be believing and baptized persons, converted to the faith by St. Peter, continuing steadfast in the Apostles' doctrine and fellowship, and in breaking of bread and in prayers. These, then, were all built upon the same rock, all professed the same faith, all received the same sacraments, all performed the same devotions, and thereby were all reputed members of the same Church. To this Church were added daily such as should be saved, who became members of the same Church by being built upon the same Foundation, by adhering to the same doctrine, by receiving the same sacraments, by performing the same devotions."

Bishop Pearson then gives six notes of unity:—

"1. Whosoever has been or ever shall be converted to the true Christian faith, are, and shall be added to that [first] Church, which is the unity of origination.

"2. They which believe the same doctrine delivered by Christ to all the Apostles, delivered by all the Apostles to believers, being all professors of the same faith, must be members of the same Church. And this is the unity of faith.

"3. All believing persons, and all Churches congregated in the name of Christ, washed in the same laver of regeneration, eating of the same bread, and drinking of the same cup, are united in the same cognisance, and so known to be the same Church. And this is the unity of the sacraments.

"4. They which depend upon the same God, and worship Him all for the same end, having all the same expectation, may well be reputed the same Church. And this is the unity of hope.

"5. They which are all of one mind, whatsoever the number of these persons be, they are in reference to that mind but one; as all the members, however different, yet being animated by one soul, become one body. Charity is of a fastening and uniting nature; nor can we call those many who endeavour to keep the unity of the Spirit in the bond of peace. By this, said our Saviour, shall all men know that ye are My disciples, if ye have love one to another. And this is the unity of charity.

"6. All the Churches of God are united into one by the unity of discipline and government, by virtue whereof the same Christ ruleth in them all. For they have all the same pastoral guides appointed, authorised, sanctified, and set apart by the appointment of God, by the direction of the Spirit, to direct and lead the people of God in the same way of eternal salvation: as, therefore, there is no Church where there is no order, no ministry; so where the same order and ministry is, there is the same Church. And this is the unity of regimen and discipline."

He adds:—"Where two or three are gathered together in the name of Christ, there is He in the midst of them, and thereby they become a Church; for they are as a builded house, and the Son within that house."

It should be remarked with regard to the sixth point of unity, that Bishop Pearson, although with all Anglican writers he insists strongly on the historical truth of episcopacy, does not further define what he deems essential to such unity of government. And the divisions amongst Christians, not separated on any of the five previous points, will be found to lie, not in their repudiation of this last note of unity, but in their opinions as to what is or is not essential to the unity of discipline and unity under Christ. Should it be a universal uniformity of organisation of all the Churches? Should it be episcopacy or presbytery, or some constitution less in accordance with the definite crystallisation of ecclesiastical development? Bishops and presbyters being in the New Testament interchangeable, is it an absolutely fatal mistake not to recognise the gradual reservation of the office and title of Bishop for those who succeeded the delegates of the Apostles?[1]

The teaching of our own Church takes up this wide view of the visible Church being a principle reproduced by aggregation to the original apostolic body at Jerusalem in countless multiplicity. "The visible Church of God is a congregation of faithful men, in the which the pure Word of God is preached, and the sacraments be duly administered according to Christ's ordinance in all those things that of necessity are requisite to the same." The first part is taken from the definition of the Council of Augsburg: "The Church is a congregation of saints in which the Gospel is rightly taught, and the sacraments are rightly administered."

[1] The Church never was *Universal* in fact; but its hopes, promises, and blessings are for all, always and everywhere; and towards this ideal its members press. *Unity* similarly is ideal, and so, alas! is holiness. Mere organic unity merely ensures a combination of office-bearers like a trades union, compatible with errors and malpractices, and tending to stereotype them, so that the times of the greatest unity have been amongst the deadest and the worst.

That which is of necessity requisite to the due administration of the sacraments is farther defined in the Church Catechism.

We have now seen what is the meaning of the Catholic faith and the word Catholic as applied to the Church. "More especially we pray," says our Prayer-book, "for the good estate of the Catholic Church; that it may be so guided and governed by Thy good Spirit, that *all who profess and call themselves Christians* may be led into the way of truth, and hold the faith in unity of spirit, in the bond of peace, and in righteousness of life." That is a true, right, and accurate ideal. Beautifully true and comprehensive also are the words of the English Bidding Prayer, the general disuse of which is greatly to be lamented: "Ye shall pray for Christ's Holy Catholic Church, that is, for *the whole congregation of Christ's people dispersed throughout the world.*"

But when well-meaning people begin to talk about a Catholic dress, a Catholic ritual, a Catholic ceremony, a Catholic custom, a Catholic collar, a Catholic candle, a Catholic building, the thing does not exist. They are talking about what is impossible. There may be dresses, rituals, ceremonies and customs of high and venerable antiquity, but there is neither dress, ritual, ceremony or custom which has been held always, everywhere, and by everybody. The rule of Vincent will hold good of truths and institutions—not of dress, ritual, and the vast majority of ceremonies and customs.

Few of these can be proved to have so august a usage. None of these, like our faith and our Church, embrace the most important factor of all, the New Testament. Baptism and the Lord's Supper are institutions attended by the very simplest of ceremonies. They are something far higher indeed. They are themselves Catholic, but the way of celebrating them has greatly varied. The descriptions of Pliny, of Justin, of the teaching of the Twelve Apostles, and even of Cyril of Jerusalem, contain the germs of what has been elsewhere developed, but they are not identical with subsequent rites.

It is in accordance with these principles that the preface to our Book of Common Prayer lays it down—

"That the particular forms of Divine worship, and the rites and ceremonies appointed to be used therein, *being things in their own nature indifferent and alterable, and so acknowledged,* it is but reasonable that, upon weighty and important considerations according to the various exigency of times and occasions, such changes and alterations should be made therein, as to those that *are in place of authority* from time to time seem either necessary or expedient."

To the same effect is the Thirty-fourth Article on the traditions of the Church—

"*It is not necessary that Traditions and Ceremonies be in all places one, or utterly like; for at all times they have been divers, and may be changed according to the diversities of countries, times, and men's manners, so that nothing be ordained against God's Word.* Whosoever through his private judgment, willingly and purposely, doth openly break the traditions and ceremonies of the Church, which be not repugnant to the Word of God, and be ordained and approved by common authority, ought to be rebuked openly (that others may fear to do the like), as he that offendeth against the common order of the Church, and hurteth the authority of the magistrate, and woundeth the consciences of the weak brethren. *Every particular or national Church hath authority to ordain, change, and abolish ceremonies or rites of the Church ordained only by man's authority, so that all things be done to edifying.*"

In the same way our Book of Common Prayer, in the Preface on Ceremonies, declares that—

"Although the keeping or omitting of a ceremony, in itself considered, is but a small thing; yet *the wilful and contemptuous transgression and breaking of a common order and discipline is no small offence before God.* 'Let all things be done among you,' saith St. Paul, 'in a seemly and due order.' The appointment of the which order pertaineth not to private men. Therefore *no man ought to take in hand, nor presume to appoint or alter any public or common order in Christ's Church, except he be lawfully called and authorised thereto.*"

And again in the same Introduction—

"Christ's Gospel is not a Ceremonial Law (as much of Moses' Law was), but it is a religion to serve God, not in bondage of the figure or shadow, but in the freedom of the Spirit; being content only with those ceremonies which do serve to a decent order and godly discipline, and such as be apt to stir up the dull mind of man to the remembrance of his duty to God, by some notable and special signification, whereby he might be edified."

And at the close of it—

"And in these our doings we condemn no other nations, nor prescribe anything but to our own people only. For *we think it convenient that every country should use such ceremonies as they shall think best to the setting forth of God's honour and glory, and to the reducing of the people to a most perfect and godly living, without error or superstition;* and that they should put away other things, which from time to time they perceive to be most abused, as in men's ordinances it often chanceth diversely in divers countries."

When, therefore, excellent and enthusiastic men go behind "*The Book of Common Prayer and Administration of the Sacraments and other Rites and Ceremonies of the Church according to the use of the Church of England*" (a title strongly to be remembered), they are not only transgressing a principle of Catholic order, that each Church should maintain its own autonomy and observe its own rites and ceremonies, and obey its own authorities without troubling about the authorities of other Churches, but they are talking of what absolutely does not exist, and is impossible. They mean only that there are certain rites and ceremonies

MEANING OF THE WORD CATHOLIC 79

which they admire, long in vogue in the Roman Communion, or Western Patriarchate, or even going back to the time before the division between East and West. They cannot show them to be really primitive. They have now been laid aside by the Church of England, which was forced in the course of time to reassert its independence. The Catholic Faith is a right term, and so is the Catholic Church. We have the right also to speak of a few simple Catholic institutions. When we come to rites, ceremonies, dresses, rituals, and customs, let us have the manliness and loyalty to recognise with our own Church that these are "things in their own nature indifferent and alterable . . . as to those that are in place of authority from time to time, seem either necessary or expedient." God grant that while we do all things decently and in order, we may have grace to turn our attention to the weightier matters of faith, hope, and charity.

V.

MEANING AND USE OF THE WORD PROTESTANT.

"The Church of England become *Protestant* at the Reformation, in order that she might be more truly and purely Catholic."
—CHRISTOPHER WORDSWORTH, Bishop of Lincoln.[1]

THE object of a name is to distinguish persons and things from others with which they might be confused. The followers of our Lord Jesus Christ were originally content to be called "the brethren," "the disciples," or "the way." They were few in number in their different neighbourhoods, and they knew what they meant by those terms. But it was not long before something more definite was required, and at Antioch a new and clearer designation grew into use. Probably their friends who did not share their change of opinions, but had no great hostility to them in consequence, invented for them the descriptive title by which they were henceforth to be known: Christ-people they were called, Christians, the followers of Christ. Nothing could be more simple and true. For a long time no other appellation was necessary. But as the heresies which the Apostles predicted grew and multiplied,

[1] *Theophilus Anglicanus*, p. 177.

MEANING OF THE WORD PROTESTANT

some further nomenclature was required. The heretics all called themselves Christians: something was needed to point out those who all over the civilised world continued united in the Apostles' fellowship and doctrine. The adoption of a name or its repudiation very often means a vast deal more than is seen on the surface. For the central body the word Catholic, or Universal, came to be employed, as we saw in the last chapter, Pacian expressing it, "Christian is my name, Catholic or Universal my surname."[1] The Universals were those who did not render themselves Particularists by some special division excluding from communion, but who everywhere held to the common doctrine of the united Churches of Christendom.

All orthodox Christians still desire to be considered in the true sense of the word Catholics or Universals, holding the clear and simple truths of the Universal Church of Christ, and continuing, as far as circumstances permit them to continue, in the Apostles' doctrine and fellowship. But at the time of the Reformation the Catholic Christians of this country were placed in a very awkward position. One of the historical developments of Christendom was the system of Patriarchates. The English Church formed part of the Patriarchate of the West, the seat of which was at Rome. The Catholic Christians of this country had become aware that, in common with the other Churches of the West, they had in the course of ages become

[1] Epist. I, *ad Sempron.*

committed to a series of most grave mistakes. The universal dominion claimed by the Western Patriarch, who had the hardihood to assert that he was the Vicar of Christ on earth, the doctrine of the Sacrifice of the Mass, the idolatrous exaltation of the mother of our Lord, the worship of saints, the worship of images, the worship of relics, the confessional, the offering of Masses for the dead, the system of Indulgences, the imprisonment of the Scriptures in a dead language, the performance of public worship in an unknown tongue, the doctrine of Transubstantiation, the enforced celibacy of the clergy, the alleged superior sanctity of the monastic life, the theory of earning salvation by works, the acceptance of tradition as the co-ordinate authority in doctrine—all these corruptions were seen to be in startling contrast with the Word of God when once it became known and understood. As the Church of Rome, to which we were subordinate, and of whose spiritual dominion we formed a part, would not reform itself, there remained no other course than for our own country to declare its independence, and to carry out the reformation in doctrine and in life for itself. Hence a new term of designation was necessary. All wished to be considered Christians. Although the unreformed Romish Churches had proceeded so far in their abuses as almost to risk the cognomen, yet it may be conceded that all desired to be Universals or Catholics by holding the principles of the Primitive Church, and by continuing in the

Apostles' doctrine and fellowship. Another vast body of Christians, the Eastern Churches and Patriarchates, had been obliged, by the arrogant pretensions of the Roman see, to break off from communion with the Western Patriarchate centuries before, and were known by the additional appellation "Orthodox." One of the most memorable scenes in all history supplied a new, honourable, and perfectly accurate name. We remained Catholic Christians in right of our appeal to Scripture, the Primitive Church, and the first four General Councils; and by our vigorous and permanent protest against the innumerable and incurable errors of Rome, we became, as distinguished from the unreformed Romanism, Catholics Protestant.

It was on April 15th, 1529,[1] at the celebrated Diet of Spires, that the Elector of Saxony, the Landgrave of Hesse, the Margrave of Brandenburg, the Prince of Anhalt, the Chancellor of Luneberg—names to be always held in grateful remembrance, together with the dignitaries of the principal towns, presented that firm and courageous document to the Imperial Commissioners which was the origin of the new description. The Emperor had taken Rome, felt himself master of the situation, and spoke out like a true Spanish despot. Two years previously the reforming princes had been forbidden to have their own public worship celebrated in churches. Now they were not even to be allowed to enjoy it in their hotels. No further reform was to

[1] *Cf.* Boultbee, XXXIX. Articles, p. 54.

be permitted, and the intention became clear of the full restoration of Popery.

"Seeing," they said, "that there is no sure doctrine but such as is conformable to the Word of God; that the Lord forbids the teaching of any other doctrine; that each text of Holy Scripture ought to be explained by other and clearer texts; and that this Holy Book is in all things necessary for the Christian easy of understanding and calculated to scatter the darkness; we are resolved, by the grace of God, to maintain the pure and exclusive teaching of His only Word, such as it is contained in the Biblical Books of the Old and New Testaments, without adding anything thereto that may be contrary to it. This Word is the only truth; it is the sure rule of all doctrine and of all life, and can never fail or deceive us. He who builds on this foundation shall stand against all the powers of hell, whilst all the human vanities that are set up against it shall fall before the face of God.

"For these reasons we earnestly entreat you to weigh carefully our grievances and our motives. If you do not yield to our request, we PROTEST by these presents before God, our only Creator, Preserver, Redeemer, and Saviour, and who will one day be our Judge, as well as before all men and all creatures, that we, for us and our people, neither consent nor adhere in any manner whatsoever to the proposed decree, in anything that is contrary to God, to His Holy Word, to our right conscience, to the salvation of our souls, and

MEANING OF THE WORD PROTESTANT

to the last decree of Spires" (which had given liberty of worship to each German state).

This celebrated Protest has well been described as one of the finest and noblest documents of Christian history, displaying an apostolic faith in Christ and Scripture, and, as far as constitutional liberties are concerned, a dignified adherence to national law. It makes a dividing line in modern Christian thought. Those who believe in the absolute authority of a mechanical ecclesiastical hierarchy, without appeal to a pure standard of Scriptural doctrine, are in point of fact on the side of Rome. Those who value the supreme authority of Holy Scripture, the rights of the individual conscience, and the witness and example of the Primitive Church are in reality Catholic Protestants.

There is a right and a wrong use of the word. It is a historical description, not a theological definition. To speak formally of the Protestant Religion would be a very inadequate conception. The Protestant Religion was a meagre term which, in the time of William the Third, Convocation, after a debate, adopted.[1] The term was too negative, and if used exclusively by itself, seemed to give up the older and still more important

---

[1] After the well-known discussions an address was agreed on by both Houses and presented to the King on Thursday, December 12, 1689. It contained the following words: "Whereby we doubt not, the interest of the Protestant religion in all other Protestant Churches, which is dear to us, will be the better secured." Rapin's "History of England," fol. 1736, vol. iii. p. 110.

cognomen, Catholic or Universal. But as a historical description it is true, and never to be repudiated.

The Act of Settlement provides that the Crown shall descend in the Protestant line.[1] In the coronation oath, drawn up by a Church of England Parliament, on the accession of William the Third and Mary, occurs the phrase, "Will you, to the utmost of your power, maintain the laws of God, the true profession of the Gospels, and the Protestant Reformed Religion established by law?" In Acts of the reign of Queen Anne, it is declared that "it is seasonable and necessary that the true Protestant religion professed and established in the Church of England, and the doctrines, worship, discipline, and government thereof, should be effectually and unalterably secured." In other Acts of Parliament the word is also employed to express "the independent attitude of the Church of England, and her distinct position from that of the Church of Rome." Every time Convocation is opened we pray at Westminster in these words: "Seeing that we all, according to the rule of our holy Reformation, have deservedly and seriously repudiated the errors, corruptions, and superstitions which formerly walked abroad in this land, and the papal tyranny, grant us firmly and with constancy to hold the Apostolic and truly Catholic faith, and to serve Thee fitly and fearlessly with a pure worship" (. . . ut qui, ad amussim

---

[1] *Cf.* Odom's "Church of England," p. 42*b*, and Church Association Tract, No. 49.

Sanctæ Reformationis nostræ, errores, corruptelas, et superstitiones olim hic grassantes, Tyrannidemque Papalem, merito et serio repudiavimus, Fidem Apostolicam et vere Catholicam firmiter et constanter teneamus omnes, Tibique rite puro cultu intrepidi serviamus). The word Protestant was formally adopted by the daughter Churches of England in the United States, "the Protestant Episcopal Churches of the United States of America," to distinguish themselves in the mind of the people from the Episcopal Churches of the Roman Communion.[1] Nowhere indeed has the attitude of true Catholic Christians towards the enormous superstitions of the unreformed Western Church been better defined than by the American bishops of our communion. "The body calling itself the Holy Roman Church has, by the decrees of the Council of Trent in 1565, and by the dogma of the Immaculate Conception in 1854, and by the decree of the Infallibility of the Pope in 1870, imposed upon the conscience of all the members of the National Churches under its sway, as of the faith to be held as of implicit necessity to salvation, dogmas having no warrant in Holy Scripture or the ancient creeds—which dogmas are so radically false as to corrupt and defile the faith; the assumption of the universal episcopate by the Bishop of Rome making operative the

---

[1] It is only on the footing of being a "Protestant" Episcopal Church that Scottish Episcopalians obtain recognition for their orders. (See Phillimore, *Eccles. Law*, p. 2221.)

definition of Papal Infallibility, has deprived of its original independence the episcopal order in the Latin Churches, and substituted for it a papal vicariate for the superintendence of dioceses; while the virtual change in the Divine constitution of the Church, as founded in the episcopate and other orders, into a Tridentine consolidation, has destroyed the autonomy, if not the corporate existence, of National Churches. Now therefore we, Bishops of the Protestant Episcopal Church in the United States of America, assembled in Council as Bishops of the Church of God, asserting the principles declared in the Lambeth Conference, and in order to the maintaining of a true unity in the truth, do hereby affirm: That the great primitive rule of the Catholic Church, 'Episcopatus unus est, cujus a singulis in solidum pars tenetur: The episcopate is one, and each unit of it is held by its different members for the making of the whole,' imposes upon the episcopates of all National Churches holding the primitive faith and order, and upon the general Bishops of the same, not the right only, but the duty also, of protecting in the holding of that faith and the recovering of that order those who, by the methods before described, have been deprived of both."

You will not be surprised to hear that the greatest writers of our National Church in the three centuries which have passed since her momentous and "holy" reformation, have used the name in its proper and truest sense with all honour and affection. The typical theologian Dean Field employs it throughout his great treatise on the Church. It is used, as a matter of course, by such men as Laud, Sancroft, Jeremy Taylor, and Atterbury. Bishop Stillingfleet grandly says, "They are Protestants who stand for the ancient and undefiled doctrine of the Catholic Church against the novel and corrupt tenets of the Roman." We may cite Dean Hook,[1] the early champion of the modern High Church movement: "We will love the Church of England, not for her Catholicism only, but for her Protestantism also; for the title of Protestant stands in antagonism, not to Catholicism, as deceivers teach, but to Romanism. We glory in our title of Protestant." Bishop Thirlwall[2] gives us a valuable testimony: "I fully sympathise," he says, "with the indignation which has been roused by the arbitrary misuse of the word 'Protestantism,' by which its meaning has been limited to a mere negation of everything that men on both sides profess to revere. But still it seems evident that those who so misuse the word can only be understood according to the sense which they themselves, however unwarrantably, attach to it, and that their meaning is perverted if what they say of Protestantism is applied to what others, in a very different sense, call the Protestant religion." Dr. Christopher Wordsworth,[3] the learned and High Church Bishop of Lincoln, wrote:

[1] Hook, *The Church and her Ordinances*, vol. i. p. 290.
[2] *Charges*, vol. i. p. 46.
[3] *Theophilus Anglicanus*, p. 177.

"The Church of England became Protestant at the Reformation, in order that she might be more truly and purely Catholic." Professor Sewell, another honoured High Churchman, wrote: "It is our glory and our happiness to be Christians; it is our safeguard and our consolation to be Catholics; our sad and melancholy duty—a duty we can never abandon till Rome has ceased to work among us—to be Protestants." A living Bishop in the south of England says: "We cannot forget the past. We protest for the pure, unadulterated truth of primitive Catholic Christianity. We protest with our Articles and Homilies against the corruptions of Rome. We protest with all our heart against any concordat or league with that fallen Church. We are Protestants, and we are not ashamed of the name." One of the most accurate, cautious, and orthodox of living theologians, Dr. Wace, has written: "Like many designations which seem to arise by accident, that word—Protestantism—is the key to the principles reasserted at the Reformation. It implies the right and the duty of the human conscience to say *No!*—to say *No* to assumptions and to claims which are inconsistent with its clear and imperative dictates—to protest against abuses, usurpations, and falsehoods, however sanctioned." And another no less recognised authority in contemporary theology (Dr. Salmon): "By Protestant I mean one who has examined into the Roman claims, and has reason to think them groundless; one who knows that there are great and precious truths on which we agree with the Church of Rome, but also points of difference so grave and fundamental as to justify our remaining in separate communion. If the Church of England be not, in this sense of the word, Protestant, her position cannot be defended at all."[1]

My brothers, you are Catholics; but unless you are Protestants also, there is no reason why you should remain in separation from the Western Patriarchate. It was a development, step by step, from the negation of those very principles which you assert. The two millions of our fellow-countrymen who adhere to the principles of that Patriarchate, tradition equal with Scripture, Episcopal authority above the individual conscience, development above the standard witness of the Primitive Church, are permitted to have their own organisation amongst us. If you are not Protestant, there it is all ready for your reception. But if you accept the principles of the English Church, do not be ashamed of that glorious history through which we have passed, and which has rescued us from spiritual darkness. You are Catholics; yes! "The creeds of Christendom speak of one Holy Catholic Apostolic Church; we claim to be the main historic branch of that Church settled these sixteen centuries past in this country, and we absolutely refuse to recognise the right of the Roman communion to claim that it alone is the Catholic Church, and that all bodies not in

[1] *Infallibility of the Church*, p. 10.

communion with it are outside its pale." But you are Protestants also. Your fathers submitted to fire, sword, and persecution to free you from the yoke of Rome. They were men of consummate learning and goodness; men, as the Archbishop of Canterbury has lately said, who would have been reckoned amongst the very greatest schoolmen of an undivided Christendom; men whose writings, as exemplified in our Book of Common Prayer, appear little short of inspired in the perfection of their beauty and their wisdom. They examined the whole system of Christianity in the calm light of experience and research, and with clear and unfaltering logic they stripped off from their consciences one superstition after another which their nurture and education had made dear and familiar. They preserved for us all that is true, and according to the mind of our Lord and His Apostles. Their work, their sufferings, their courage, their learning have made the way plain for us, and won us our liberties, temporal and spiritual. It is foolish, ungrateful, and unworthy to affect to disparage their position, and to disclaim their standpoint. It is true that the word Protestant has been misused. Some who have hardly any title to be called Christians at all, style themselves by that honoured designation, and assume that we all stand on the same general principles of Protest against what they term the tyranny of Churches and creeds. It is true that we ought not to forget the warning of Edmund Burke against the spirit of mere denial: " A man certainly is the most perfect Protestant who protests against the whole Christian religion. The countenance given from a spirit of controversy to that negative religion, may by degrees encourage light and unthinking people to a total indifference to everything positive in matters of doctrine, and, in the end, of practice too. If continued, it would play the game of that sort of active proselytising and persecuting atheism which is the disgrace and calamity of our time." But the wrong use of an important word must not be allowed to injure the use which is right. Unless you accept the designation, which would express the inestimable truths which it implies,[1] or some equivalent, there is no trustworthy barrier that you can raise between your own vague religious ideas and aspirations and the surrounding ideas of Rome. There is a zealous and hard-working body of men, not well instructed in these important and necessary distinctions, who, with a certain light-hearted frivolity, pour ridicule upon our inherited distinction, and disparage the Reformation. They are really giving up the citadel of our position. Strong in the intrenched fortress of the authoritative and recognised documents of our National Church, you

[1] Among the positive beliefs characteristic of Protestantism are immediate access to the throne of grace, the Real Presence of Christ in the individual, both in and out of the use of special ordinances, direct communion with the Saviour, present possession of an assured hope working from, not to, salvation, immediate action of the Divine Spirit on the human spirit, not *viâ* inspired elements. These cut away the supposed necessity of sacrifices, confessionals, and go-betweens of every description.

can accept their unwise raillery with unperturbed patience. You can read their ill-considered sneers with the unruffled good-humour worthy of an impregnable and true historical standpoint. Never mind whether the name is for the moment popular or not. It is true, it is important, it is necessary. It is for you, by the earnestness of your faith, the warmth of your love, the zeal of your self-sacrifice, to vindicate it once more in the face of the people. And by your forbearance, your good sense, your loyalty, your knowledge, your recognition of the facts of the case, your enthusiasm for truth, your absolute obedience to your Lord and Master, you will in the end convince these merry jesters that their estimate is mistaken, their sympathies misplaced, their history misconceived, and their position untenable. Well has it been said by a writer from whom I have already quoted:[1] "If the Church of England is to continue as a National Church, and to be an increased power and glory in the country, it must be in the fullest sense at once Catholic and Protestant —upholding and teaching Apostolic doctrine, and protesting against superstition and error." The warning words must not be lightly regarded: " When the clergy abjure their Protestantism they will abjure all sympathy with one of the primary movements of English life; their Church will cease to be the Church of England, and they will sink into the condition of an ultramontane priesthood amidst a contemptuous laity."

[1] The Rev. W. Odom, "The Church of England."

VI.

A PLEA FOR FORBEARANCE IN DISAGREEMENT.

"Those parties which in Newman's time were dominant, and which, ever since the Reformation, had enabled a large, if not the larger, portion of the nation to remain within the pale of the Anglican Church, were now, it would seem, so far as the clergy were concerned, to be turned out."[1]

SPEAKING in Convocation in 1864, on the difficult question of the discipline of the Colonial Churches, and of the determined line taken by Bishop Gray, the Metropolitan of South Africa, Dr. Tait, who was then Bishop of London, said, "I consider him to hold very strong opinions on one side, differing from myself and much more than half of the Bishops of the Church of England. He is fully entitled to hold these opinions; but I think there is this fault in his character, that he is not content with merely holding these opinions, but that he wishes to make every other person hold them too."[2] It is an inseparable characteristic of any earnest and conscientious theological movement that its adherents should desire to influence by every means in

[1] Abbot's "Anglican Career of Cardinal Newman," vol. i. p. 325, on "Laicus and Clericus" in the "Via Media."
[2] "Life of Archbishop Tait," i. 361.

their power the opinions of others in their own direction; and there is also the tendency, as time goes on, and new circumstances develop, or new suggestions are made, to adopt rules of conduct and thought, increasing in strictness and in their claim to obedience. The leaders of such movements have always been in the habit of telling us that a certain new restriction is part of their system, a certain new action a necessary corollary of their principles. And if in any such theological movement there be the same arbitrary character, it may be very necessary for those who are jealous for religious truth to scan it very closely.

Without going back to the tyrannical absurdities of the Puritan days, which led to a licentious reaction at the Restoration, something of this sort might have been observable in parts of the older Evangelical movement. No sermon was complete if it did not contain the doctrine of justification by faith, or if it did not repeat certain favourite theological phrases; it was wrong to dance, wrong to go to a concert. Cards, novels, and many other debatable forms of amusement were forbidden. Life became too much restricted, and the result was that from some of the purest and holiest homes of the Evangelicals came, by a violent reaction, the most reckless and abandoned of profligates. Now, this is only the old contrast reappearing between the spirit of the law and the spirit of the Gospel. It was not to the law as such that St. Paul objected, as to a servile bondage to its letter regarded as the ideal of a fulfilled

righteousness. "Where the Spirit of the Lord is," he says, "there is liberty."[1] "The glorious liberty of the children of God"[2] is the aim at which all creation is striving. "Stand fast," he says to another Church, "in the liberty wherewith Christ has made us free, and be not entangled again with the yoke of bondage."
"If ye be dead," he writes to another Church, "with Christ from the rudiments of the world, why, as though living in the world, are ye subject to ordinances (touch not; taste not; handle not; which all are to perish with the using), after the commandments and doctrines of men?"[4] "Who art thou," he says to the Romans, "that judgest another man's servant? to his own master he standeth or falleth. Yea, he shall be holden up, for God shall keep him."[5] "One man esteemeth one day above another; another esteemeth every day alike; let every man be fully persuaded in his own mind. He that regardeth the day, to the Lord he regardeth it; and he that regardeth not the day, to the Lord he doth not regard it. Why dost thou judge thy brother? why dost thou set at nought thy brother? for it is before the judgment seat of Christ that we shall all stand."[6] St. James also speaks of "the perfect law of liberty," and urges his friends: "So speak ye, and so do, as they that shall be judged by the law of liberty."[7] This, in short, is one of the most characteristic features of the Gospel of Christ.

[1] 2 Cor. iii. 17.   [2] Rom. viii. 21.   [3] Gal. v. 1.   [4] Col. ii. 20.
[5] Rom. xiv. 4.   [6] Ibid. ver. 5.   [7] James i. 25.

Our religion is a matter primarily between our own conscience and God. Whatever ordinances are introduced in order to enable men to live in a Christian society, they must always be subject to this ideal, and infringe it as little as may be possible. It is curious that Calvin, who himself was the author of the most rigid theoretical system to which human intellect and conduct have ever been subjected, saw the force of this teaching of the Apostles. "Certainly," he says, speaking of spiritual liberty, "it is an invaluable blessing, in defence of which it is our duty to fight, even to death. If men lay upon our shoulders an unjust burden, it may be borne, but if they endeavour to bring our conscience into bondage, we must resist valiantly, even to death; if men be permitted to bind our consciences, we shall be deprived of an invaluable blessing, and an insult will be at the same time offered to Christ, the Author of our freedom."

> This is a liberty unsung,
> By poets and by senators unpraised,
> Which monarchs cannot grant, nor all the powers
> Of earth and hell confederate take away;
> A liberty, which persecution, fraud,
> Oppression, prisons have no power to bind,
> Which whoso tastes can be enslaved no more.
> 'Tis liberty of heart, derived from Heaven,
> Bought with His blood, who gave it to mankind.

. . . . . .

> The oppresser holds
> His body bound; he knows not what a range

> His spirit takes unconscious of the chain ;
> And that to bind him, is a vain attempt,
> Whom God delights in, and in whom He dwells ![1]

The contrast between the absolutely free ideal of the Christian Church and the simple regulations which enable its members to carry out its objects on the earth is admirably drawn out by Bishop Lightfoot.[2] "The kingdom of Christ," he says, "not being a kingdom of this world, is not limited by the restrictions which fetter other societies, political or religious. It is in the fullest sense free, comprehensive, universal. It displays this character, not only in the acceptance of all comers who seek admission irrespective of race, or caste, or sex, but also in the instruction and treatment of those who are already its members. It has no sacred days or seasons, and no special sanctuaries, because every time and every place alike are holy. Above all, it has no sacerdotal system. It interposes no sacrificial tribe or class between God and man, by whose intervention alone God is reconciled and man forgiven. Each individual, therefore, holds personal communion with the Divine Head. To Him immediately he is responsible, and from Him directly he obtains pardon and draws strength. It is most important that we should keep this ideal definitely in view, and I have therefore stated it as broadly as possible. Yet the broad statement, if allowed to stand

---

[1] Cowper.
[2] Epistle to the Philippians, "Christian Ministry," p. 179.

alone, would suggest a false impression, or at least would convey only a half truth. It must be evident that no society of men could hold together without officers, without rules, without institutions of any kind; and the Church of Christ is not exempt from this universal law. The conception, in short, is strictly an ideal which we must ever hold before our eyes, which should inspire and interpret ecclesiastical polity, but which nevertheless cannot supersede the necessary wants of human society, and, if crudely and hastily applied, will only lead to signal failure. . . . In this respect the ethics of Christianity present an analogy to the politics. Here, also, the ideal conception and the actual realisation are incommensurate, and in a manner contradictory. The Gospel is contrasted with the law as the spirit with the letter. Its ethical principle is not a code of positive ordinances, but conformity to a perfect exemplar, incorporation into a divine life. The distinction is most important, and eminently fertile in practical results. Yet no man would dare to live without laying down more or less definite rules for his own guidance, without yielding obedience to law in some sense; and those who discard or attempt to discard all such aids are often farthest from the attainment of Christian perfection." "This qualification," continues Bishop Lightfoot, "is introduced here to deprecate any misunderstanding to which the opening statement, if left without compensation, would fairly be exposed. . . . In attempting to investigate the historical development of the Divine institution, no better starting-point suggested itself than the characteristic distinction of Christianity, as declared occasionally by the direct language, but more frequently by the eloquent silence of the Apostolic writings."

This position of Bishop Lightfoot is in absolute harmony with the teaching of Scripture; and its lesson is obvious. Whatever arrangements may be necessary for human co-operation in the kingdom of God, they must be of the very simplest and most elementary character, jealously guarded against any infringement of the ideal of Christian liberty. Now we are in the presence of an ecclesiastical phenomenon of the very highest interest. The last half-century of the life of the National Church of England has been characterised by a religious movement of the most zealous and successful description. The late Dean of St. Paul's, in his last and posthumous work, ends it by speaking of the days after the sad secessions of 1845: "Those times," he says, "were the link between what we are now, so changed in many ways, and the original impulse given at Oxford; but to those times I am as much an outsider as most of the foremost in them are outsiders to Oxford in the earlier days. Those times are almost more important than the history of the movement, for besides vindicating it, they carried on its work to achievements and successes which, even in the most sanguine days of 'Tractarianism,' had not presented themselves to men's minds, much less to their hopes."[1]

These words of Dean Church are nothing less than the fact. The spread of the movement of which he is the historian is one of the most marked features of contemporary life. We read, for instance, that at the thirty-fourth anniversary of the English Church Union, besides some twenty-nine bishops, the Union has 34,761 names on the books, of whom 4200 are in holy orders. We read the other day of the thirty-first anniversary of the Confraternity of the Blessed Sacrament. The report shows a steady increase of members, lay and clerical, at home and abroad. There are now more than 15,000 members, of whom more than 1600 are priests; there are 300 wards in England and Wales, and twenty-two abroad. Among the objects for which this society prays are the restoration of the "primitive" custom of reserving the Blessed Sacrament, the cessation of evening Communion, the spread of auricular confession, and prayer for the repose of the souls of those who are dead. Another characteristic society is that of the Holy Cross, and, again, a fifth is the well-known Association for Promoting the Unity of Christendom. The spread of these vast societies is an indication of that wonderful growth and development of the original movement of which Dean Church speaks. It is not my purpose on the present occasion to inquire into the teaching connected with this movement, or to suggest whether or

[1] "The Oxford Movement," 1833-1845, p. 352.

not it has contravened those simple principles and rules by which Bishop Lightfoot says bodies of Christians may properly be united. My wish is to point out, in the first place, that the movement has taken a very large measure of liberty to itself. Secondly, that to all new movements application may be made of the remark of Bishop Tait on Bishop Gray, that "he was not content with holding his own opinions, but was anxious to make everybody else hold them too." Thirdly, that many opinions associated with the later developments of the movement are in some degree inconsistent with the Christian liberty of those who neither belong to it nor agree with it; and that, fourthly, there is for such persons ample security for such Christian liberty in the authoritative and integral formularies of the English Church, if they are only suitably used and maintained.

First, I shall enumerate very briefly the points where the movement in question appears itself to depend on a considerable use of the principle of liberty. And, indeed, I do not think that there is any great desire on the part of the great body of the National Church to curtail such freedom. Archbishop Tait long ago pointed out that the Church of Andrewes, Cosin, Bull, and Bramhall would naturally contain a section which would hold high views of the meaning of the Sacraments and of ministerial succession and authority. In another place he says, "The Church of England from the Reformation has allowed great liberty as to the doctrine of the

Sacraments; and though I fear it cannot be denied that a few men are engaged in a conspiracy to bring back our Church to the state in which it was before the Reformation, I fully believe that most of those who advocate what we deem an excessive ritual would indignantly deny any such purpose."[1] And again, "The Church of England is very wide, embracing persons of very various opinions within the limits of our common faith; and the Episcopal bench would not be a true representative of the Church, if within our own body there was not that variance of sentiment in minor matters which exists in the Church itself." And again, in 1866, "The Church of England," he says, "does allow amongst its people great diversity of opinion in non-essentials. This is a necessary characteristic of a Protestant branch of the Church Catholic. Sects of all kinds, whether Protestant or so-called Catholic, are narrow and unwarrantably dogmatic, defining where God's Word has not defined, eager to exclude from their pale all who will not allow their minds to be forced into one groove. Such the Church of England has never been, through any continuous period of its history, though at certain epochs many efforts have been made, and for a time succeeded in endeavouring to narrow it to the dimensions of a sect."[2]

This view, I believe, is generally prevalent in the great body of the National Church, and in enumerating the points in which it appears that the mediæval

[1] "Life of Archbishop Tait," vol. i. p. 442.   [2] Ibid. vol. i. p. 482.

movement has depended upon a wide application of the principle of liberty, I repeat that I am not here questioning how far that liberty ought to extend. And I do not mean that all those who are affected by the movement agree in all such points. There is a great variety of opinion within the movement, and some would repudiate one point, some another. But at any rate, among such points are those of "the sacrifice of the altar," the sacrificial priesthood, the exclusion of Presbyterian Churches from the Church of Christ, instead of treating them as, from the Episcopalian point of view, defective branches; the principle that the members of any Church which has Apostolical succession may borrow the practices of other Churches, whether they have been adopted or not, or forbidden or not, by their own National Church; the distinction between low celebrations, when persons are supposed to communicate, and high celebrations, when they are not; the provision of prayers suitable to these two distinctions; the setting up of tradition as of equal authority with Scripture, or of even greater importance; the assumption that during the forty days between our Lord's resurrection and ascension He handed over a number of doctrines to His Apostles, of which there is no subsequent trace in the Epistles, and which only reappear in the development of the Church subsequent to the death of the Apostles; the adoration of the Eucharist, the elevation of the cup and of the paten, prayers for the dead, and especially celebrations for the dead on All Souls' Day; the invocation of saints, and in many cases a direct worship of the Virgin Mary. It would be possible to enumerate other points, but these are enough to prove my assertion that the later developments of the movement do depend very largely on the principle of liberty; these opinions and practices are now very general, and receive no check of any kind.

I now proceed with the second point, that the movement, like other new and earnest developments, is not conspicuous for toleration of divergent opinions. The universal practice of its adherents is to speak of themselves and their friends as *good Churchmen*, or still more exclusively as *Churchmen*, while to others they deny this description. The catechism largely used by the Church Extension Society treats dissent as a mortal sin, and implies that Nonconformists are outside the pale of salvation. The organs of the movement, which are very powerful, ignore to a large extent the influence and work of the older sections of the Church, and confine themselves mainly to the propagation of the opinions of the movement. One of the organs of the movement declares unreservedly that its object is to unprotestantise, if possible, the Church of England, and to bring back and enthrone in her high places the doctrines which she so distinctly repudiated and cast out at the time of the Reformation. A prominent and favourite teacher in the movement earnestly desires that the Bible may once more be confined to the hands of an authorised priesthood. "There are a great many persons," says another, "who are under the impression that the Bible is intended to teach us our religion; let me say most distinctly that this is a great mistake." One of the "Tracts for the Times" taught that Scripture does not interpret itself; tradition is practically infallible, and has revealed truth not contained in the Bible. In their great zeal for uniformity of practice, they strongly condemn the Scriptural habit of evening Communion. The cessation of this habit is, as I before mentioned, one of the objects of intercession of the Confraternity of the Blessed Sacrament. "There is no foundation," writes an excellent friend of mine, "in Holy Scripture for the innovation of evening Communion." Any person who maintains that fasting Communion is unnecessary, incurs their severest reprobation. The doctrine of justification by faith itself, which may be considered the leading characteristic of Pauline and English Christianity, appears to excite their opposition. "The doctrine of justification by faith," wrote one of their most popular preachers, "is a delusive figment." It can, indeed, hardly be denied that the aim of the movement is in a very large degree the extinction of those principles which differentiate the reformed Church of England from the un-reformed Church of the Middle Ages. "What, we should like to know," wrote one of the organs of the movement, "is the Church of England to do with those members who are guided by the spirit of the reformers, but to get rid of them as soon as possible?

We will have nothing to do with such a set." "We have never seen the use," writes another of their organs, "of retaining the Thirty-nine Articles." The movement is, in short, very candid, frank, and open, as well as ceaselessly earnest and energetic; it has a very definite polemical object in view, and it makes no secrets of its aims.

Now, while we hold and are able to hold our own faith in simplicity and loyalty and perfect independence, we are bound, I think, to protect the liberty of those whose principles it appears it is desired to extinguish. The "Oxford Movement," as it is called by Dean Church, is decidedly not stationary. It is on the increase; it is largely recruited every Ember week from many of those who leave the theological colleges. The leaders of the movement would not like disestablishment at the present moment, because the old adherents of the National Church in England would probably be strong enough to retain our existing formularies, being as they are a protest against those mediæval doctrines, which at the time of the Reformation were summed up in the one word—Rome. But if they had another quarter or half century, they would look forward in that case to being strong enough to reorganise the Church of England on their own principles, and to sweep away those traces of the Reformation which they so greatly dislike. It is our duty, then, I say, in every way to protect and strengthen those who hold by the old Scriptural standard of the reformed Church of England. It is useless to pretend that our Church does not deserve the name of Protestant. It is a name of which we ought all to be proud; and there is no need to shrink from using it, when occasion arises, in our sermons, teachings, and conversation. The whole position of the Church of England, as apart from its Catholic setting forth of the old Scriptural verities, is a protest against mediæval error; and we must not allow any fallacy to creep in as to the use of the word Rome, as distinct from mediæval. The reformers used the word Rome as a summary of all error, because Rome embraced the whole Western Church. It is common now amongst the adherents of the mediæval movement to profess that they have nothing to do with Rome, but that they only follow Sarum. This is a mere fallacy, for Sarum was in truth more Roman than Rome itself. The truly wise position for English Christians was laid down by Archbishop Tait, when he wrote, "Since the Church of England is not only Catholic, as holding the old faith, but also Protestant, there are essentials not of the Christian faith, but of our charter, as reformed from Roman error, which it is equally vain for any man to hope that he can with a safe conscience ignore."[1]

We saw in the last chapter that by the Coronation Oath the sovereign, as temporal ruler of the Church, is sworn to maintain the Protestant reformed religion, established by law; and, according to the Act of

[1] "Life," vol. i. p. 483.

Settlement of 1688, the occupant of the throne of Great Britain must not only be a Protestant, but can only marry a Protestant. Instead of allowing any other authority parallel to Scripture, we must point out the 6th Article, as, in these days, the very palladium of Christian liberty in England: "Holy Scripture containeth all things necessary to salvation, so that whatsoever is not read therein, nor may be proved thereby, is not to be required of any man, that it should be believed as an article of the faith, or be thought requisite or necessary to salvation." Protestantism, in fact, far from being a bare negation, is the assertion of a living principle, the absolute supremacy of the Word of God, and the inalienable right of all men to search that Word.

Again, when it is desired strictly to exclude orthodox Presbyterian Churches from the Church of Christ, instead of treating them as defective branches, while we fully maintain the practical importance of historical succession, we must point to the notes of the Church in the 19th Article: "The visible Church of Christ is a congregation of faithful men, in the which the pure Word of God is preached and the Sacraments be duly administered, according to Christ's ordinance, in all those things which of necessity are requisite to the same." And we shall quote such a passage as the following from Hooker: "Now, whereas some do infer that no ordination can stand, but only such as is made by Bishops, which have had their ordination likewise from other Bishops before them, till we come to the very Apostles themselves. . . . To this we answer that there may be sometimes a very just and sufficient reason to allow ordination made without a Bishop. The whole Church visible being the true original subject of all power, it hath not ordinarily allowed any other than Bishops alone to ordain: howbeit as the ordinary course is ordinarily in all things to be observed, so it may be in some cases not unnecessary that we decline from those ordinary ways. Men may be extraordinarily, yet allowably, in two ways admitted into spiritual functions in the Church. One is when God Himself doth of Himself raise up any, whose labour He useth without requiring that men should authorise them. . . . Another extraordinary kind of vocation is when the exigence of necessity doth constrain to leave the usual ways of the Church, which otherwise we would willingly keep, where the Church must needs have some ordained, and neither hath nor can have possibly a Bishop to ordain; in case of such necessity, the ordinary institution of God hath given oftentimes, and may give place. And, therefore, we are not simply without exception to urge a lineal descent of power from the Apostles by continued succession of Bishops in every effective ordination." [1]

I cite another very important passage from Field, "On the Church," in his controversy with Bellarmine: "There is no reason to be given but that in case of

[1] Hooker, *Eccl. Pol.*, VII., xiv. 11.

necessity, wherein all Bishops were extinguished by death, or, being fallen into heresy, should refuse to ordain any to serve God in His true worship, but that Presbyters, as they may do all other acts . . . might do this also. Who, then, dare condemn all those worthy ministers of God that were ordained by Presbyters, in sundry Churches of the world, at such times as Bishops, in those parts where they lived, opposed themselves against the truth of God, and persecuted such as professed it?"[1] Two more witnesses to Christian liberty I will cite—Archbishop Laud and Bishop Cosin. Archbishop Laud, in his conference with Fisher the Jesuit, denounces the necessity of continued visible succession, or the existence of any promise that it should be uninterruptedly continued in any Church. He proceeds to say: "That for succession in the general I shall say this—it is a great happiness where it may be had, visible and continued, and a great conquest over the mutability of this present world. But I do not find any one of the ancient Fathers that makes local, personal, visible, and continued succession a necessary mark, or sign, of the true Church in any one place."[2] Then for Bishop Cosin. He severely censures, indeed, the Protestant Churches of France and Geneva for their defect of episcopacy, but he says, "I dare not take upon me to condemn or declare nullity of their own ordinations against them." He further acknowledges

---

[1] Field, "On the Church," bk iii. chap. xxxix.
[2] Section XXXIX. vii.

that in the face of certain passages in St. Jerome, some schoolmen, Jewell, Field, Hooker, and others, he cannot say that the ministers of the Reformed French Churches, for want of episcopal ordination, have no order at all, but recommends his correspondent to communicate with the French Protestants rather than with the Roman Church.[1]

Once more as to the authority of General Councils. In Tract No. 90, Newman tries to persuade himself that some of the General Councils were not an assembly of mere men, but were truly of heavenly inspiration, and therefore do not come under the teaching of our 21st Article; and it is a favourite practice of the adherents of the mediæval movement to select some canon from any ancient Council which happens to suit their purpose, and to quote it as the authorised legislation of Christendom, which, if treated with indifference by any member of the National English Church, will stamp him at once as unorthodox. Those who know the history of General Councils are aware that not one of them was representative of the whole of Christendom, that many of their decrees are mistaken, that their results were not at once accepted, while the most important of them only gradually gained acceptance by their evident agreement with the Bible. And again, therefore, we cling with the utmost gratitude to the 21st Article, which says of General Councils: "That when they be gathered together, forasmuch as they be

[1] See Goode's "Divine Rule of Faith," vol. ii. p. 293, 2nd ed.

an assembly of men, whereof all be not governed with the Spirit and Word of God, they may err, and sometimes have erred, even in things pertaining unto God; wherefore things ordained by them as necessary to salvation have neither strength nor authority unless it may be declared that they be taken out of Holy Scripture (ostendi possint)."

Lastly, we must defend the duty of English Christianity to maintain the doctrine of the one oblation of Christ finished upon the cross, and never to be repeated. The teaching which is very generally given by adherents of the mediæval movement is contained in the second chapter of the twenty-second session of the Council of Trent. It is in the following words: "Since the same Christ who once offered Himself by His blood on the cross is contained in this Divine sacrifice, which is celebrated in the mass and offered without blood, the Holy Synod teaches that this sacrifice is really propitiatory. . . . For assuredly God, appeased by this oblation, bestows grace and the gift of repentance, and forgives all crimes and sins how great soever; for by the ministry of the priests the victim is one and the same, the same now offering who then offered it on the cross, only the mode of offering is different. And the fruits of that bloody oblation are plentifully enjoyed by means of this unbloody one."

The language in the canon of the Council of Trent in nowise differs from the language of the adherents of the Oxford movement, when in their eight or nine hundred churches they return thanks to Almighty God for being permitted to offer unto Him Christ's perpetually pleaded sacrifice. The fact is, that as praise, almsgiving, and self-devotion are called sacrifices in the New Testament, the word "sacrifice" and the word "altar" became used in very early times in connection with the Lord's Supper. And these words having been once introduced, and having come into ordinary usage, suffer the usual fate of ambiguities. With the progress of doctrinal corruption the idea of expiatory sacrifice offered by the priest on the altar came in; and as with the doctrine of Transubstantiation, so with this. After centuries of oscillating and contradictory language, the doctrine of the propitiatory sacrifice of the Eucharist became generally prevalent. Waterland, in a very important chapter (the twelfth) enumerates eight true and evangelical sacrifices:—

1. The sacrifice of alms to the poor, and oblations to the Church.
2. The sacrifice of prayer.
3. The sacrifice of praise.
4. The sacrifice of a true heart.
5. The sacrifice of ourselves.
6. The sacrifice by the Church of itself to Christ.
7. The offering up of true converts by their minister.
8. The sacrifice of faith, hope, and self-humiliation in commemorating the death of Christ.[1]

It is very difficult to see how anything could be

[1] Waterland, "Doctrine of the Eucharist," chap. xii.

more explicit than our 31st Article: "The offering of Christ once made is the perfect redemption, propitiation, and satisfaction for all the sins of the whole world, both original and actual; and there is no other satisfaction for sin but that alone. Wherefore the sacrifices of masses, in the which it was commonly said that the priests did offer Christ for the quick and the dead to have remission of pain or guilt, were blasphemous fables and dangerous deceits."

As long as our clergy are bound by this Article, the great body of the National Church who adhere to the Reformation are beyond all question protected in their Christian duty of understanding the sacrifice in the Communion Service according to the teaching of Holy Scripture. It would be easy to point out other grounds for liberty; but it only remains that we should properly maintain and use these safeguards. It is very unpleasant, no doubt, to be mixed up in controversy, and to be combating error; but we can, at any rate, urge the friends of the Reformation to understand their own position and its unassailable strength. And by the firmness of our attitude, the gentleness of our charity, and the width of our toleration, we can persuade our friends—who, in all their earnestness and zeal and self-devotion, are proceeding so far in restoring the mediæval and traditional standards to which the Scriptural standards of the Reformation are opposed—that the other side of the question has more right to the claim of orthodox English churchmanship than themselves; and we can satisfy them that whatever they do in their own Churches, and with their own flocks, they have no reason to be surprised if the rest of English Christians are firm in their resolve to stand fast *in the liberty wherewith Christ has made them free.* I will conclude with the words used by Archbishop Tait, when preaching at the consecration of All Saints', Margaret Street. "I truly believe," he said, "that in these days, both amongst High Church and Low Church, there are persons who are tired of the miserable controversies which have long divided Christendom, and who simply desire, while using the liberty allowed them, to follow their own tastes in things indifferent, to worship the Lord Jesus Christ faithfully, and to follow Him in their lives. Beware, lest in your zeal for antiquity, you would be not ancient enough, going back to the wavering followers of the Apostles, and not to the Apostles themselves."[1]

[1] "Life of Archbishop Tait," vol. i. p. 421.

VII.

OUR UNHAPPY DIVISIONS.

"Be ye all of one mind, having compassion one of another, love as brethren, be pitiful, be courteous: not rendering evil for evil, . . . but contrariwise blessing."—1 PET. iii. 8, 9.

WE must all, I think, be inclined to add to our prayers at this time the comment written on these words by an illustrious Christian, Robert Hall:—"Could we indulge the hope that such a oneness of mind was likely soon to establish itself, we should hail the dawn of a brighter day, and consider it as a nearer approach to the ultimate triumph of the Church of Christ than the annals of time have yet recorded. In the accomplishment of our Lord's prayer that all His people may be one, men would behold a demonstration of the Divinity of His mission which the most impious could not resist, and would behold in the Church a peaceful haven inviting them to retire from the tossings and perils of this unquiet ocean to a sacred enclosure, a sequestered spot, which the storms and tempests of the world were not permitted to invade." Ah! how piteous it is to look round about in the world for this ideal. When we repeat in our Creed our belief in the Holy Catholic

Church, how heartrending it is to remember the deep dividing lines which cut the members of Christ asunder! The estimated population of the earth is one thousand, four hundred and seventy-nine millions.[1] Of that vast number only three hundred and ninety-three millions, not so much as a quarter, are even nominally Christian. Of these by far the larger portion—more than half—are adherents of the Church of Rome, which excommunicates the rest. The Church of Rome is said to have no less than one hundred and ninety millions of followers. Next comes the ancient Orthodox Greek Church of the East, the Church which gave us the Nicene Creed, the Church which (indirectly) sent Christianity to the Britons before the arrival of the Roman mission of Augustine to the Anglo-Saxons. The Greek Church is said to number eighty-four millions. Next in proportion would rank our own National Church of England, with the Reformed Episcopalian Churches which are in full communion with us throughout the world. We and they are estimated at some twenty-three millions, not much more than a quarter of the Greek Church, not much more than an eighth of that Roman Communion, which arrogates to itself the title of the Catholic Church. The Reformed Churches and sects which do not follow the episcopal form of government are reckoned to be ninety-three millions—more in numbers than the Greek Church, but not more than half of the subjects of the Pope of Rome.

[1] Hazell's *Annual*, p. 573.

If it were not for the tragedy of it, Christendom would present an aspect only too like the celebrated scene in Sheridan's famous comedy, where the father scolds the hero, the hero curses the valet, and the valet kicks the page. The one hundred and ninety millions of Romanists excommunicate the eighty-four millions of the Greek Church and the one hundred and sixteen millions of Reformed Christians. The Greek Church cannot officially recognise the twenty-three millions of English and other Episcopalians, because we have added a single clause to the creed of Constantinople or Nicæa. And although our own Church has always taken up the most comprehensive and charitable attitude, yet there are, no doubt, many amongst us who feel little sympathy for the purely Protestant communions, and who look askance at the manifold ramifications of Protestant Nonconformity. The National Church of Scotland, again, believing that presbyters and bishops were originally one and the same, declines to be classed with the Nonconforming communions. And these other communions are now separated into some two hundred and fifty divergent divisions. Split up by these wretched mistakes and quarrels, we Christians stand this day before Almighty God, after nineteen centuries of storm and sunshine, of sin and forgiveness, side by side with eight millions of Jews, one hundred and seventy millions of Mohammedans, and the appalling aggregate of more than nine hundred millions of heathens. To Him who has left us in His Holy Word that message of gracious peace—" Be ye all of one mind, having compassion one of another, love as brethren, be pitiful, be courteous, not rendering evil for evil . . . but contrariwise blessing"—we cannot but cry with bowed head and broken voice:—" Almighty and most merciful Father; we have erred, and strayed from Thy ways like lost sheep. We have followed too much the devices and desires of our own hearts. We have offended against Thy holy laws. We have left undone those things which we ought to have done; and we have done those things which we ought not to have done; and there is no health in us."

We cannot help asking what is our duty under these painful circumstances. With regard to the Roman Church, our position has been rendered very clear by themselves. They deny our Orders, and ridicule our pretension to be a Church at all. They consider it a mortal sin for a Romanist even to kneel down and say the Lord's Prayer with one who is outside their pale. They have directly excommunicated all who do not submit to the Pope as the Vicar of Christ. Our attitude towards such tyrannical exclusiveness has been very properly defined by the Bishops of the United States of America. Their important declaration has already been quoted on p. 80. In 1878 the Official Letter of the Bishops of the Lambeth Conference spoke as follows:—

"The fact that a solemn protest is raised in so many Churches and Christian communities throughout the world against the usurpations of the See of Rome, and against the novel doctrines promulgated by its authority, is a subject for thankfulness to Almighty God. All sympathy is due from the Anglican Church to the Churches and individuals protesting against these errors, and labouring, it may be, under special difficulties, from the assaults of unbelief as well as from the pretensions of Rome.

"We acknowledge but one Mediator between God and men—the Man Christ Jesus, who is over all, God blessed for ever. We reject, as contrary to the Scriptures and to Catholic truth, any doctrine which would set up other mediators in His place, or which would take away from the Divine Majesty of the fulness of the Godhead which dwelleth in Him, and which gave an infinite value to the spotless sacrifice which He offered, once for all, on the Cross for the sins of the whole world.

"It is therefore our duty to warn the faithful that the act done by the Bishop of Rome, in the Vatican Council, in the year 1870—whereby he asserted a supremacy over all men in matters both of faith and morals, on the ground of an assumed infallibility—was an invasion of the attributes of the Lord Jesus Christ."[1]

And in 1888 a Report of the Lambeth Conference uses the following language of the Old Catholic movement:—

[1] Davidson's "Lambeth Conferences," p. 181

"We cannot consider that it is in schism as regards the Roman Church, because to do so would be to concede the lawfulness of the imposition of new terms of communion, and of the extravagant assertions by the Papacy of ordinary and immediate jurisdiction in every Diocese. For ourselves we regard it as a duty to promote friendly relations with the Old Catholics of Germany, not only out of sympathy with them, but also in thankfulness to God, who has strengthened them to suffer for the truth under great discouragements, difficulties, and temptations. We owe them our intercessions, our support, and our brotherly counsel; and we have reason to believe that aid from individual members of our Church may be most beneficially given towards the training of their future clergy."[1]

There are in Great Britain some two millions of Roman Catholics. We do not grudge them their own organisation. We can co-operate with them in all good works where we are not asked to compromise our principles. But we must not pretend to be blind to their mistakes both in morals and doctrines. And while we patiently hope and humbly pray that this, so immensely the largest section of the Christian Church, will in God's own good time be brought to a better mind, we cannot properly forget that by them we have been absolutely and entirely excommunicated.

[1] Davidson's "Lambeth Conferences," p. 342.

It is more practical for us to turn our attention to the next question. What is our relation to the Nonconformist communions of our own country, England? The population of England is upwards of twenty-nine millions. The adherents of the National Church are reckoned at about fifteen millions. Deducting two millions for the Papists, we find there are about nine millions belonging to other bodies. The largest denomination of these are the Wesleyan Methodists, the next the Independents, the third the Baptists. With regard to these, fellow-Christians with ourselves, what should be our conduct?

First, we must remember what many are inclined to ignore, that important difference laid down by our typical English theologian, Hooker, between the invisible Church of Christ and that which is visible: "That Church of Christ (says Hooker, in a well-known passage) which we properly term His body mystical, can be but one, neither can that one be sensibly discerned by any man, inasmuch as the parts thereof are some in heaven already with Christ, and the rest that are on earth (albeit their natural persons be visible) we do not discern under this property whereby they are truly and infallibly of that body. Only our minds, by intellectual imagination, are able to apprehend that such a body there is—a body collective, because it containeth a huge multitude; a body mystical, because the mystery of their conjunction is removed altogether from sense. Whatsoever we read in Scripture concerning the endless love and the saving mercy which God showeth towards His Church, the only proper subject thereof is this (invisible) Church. Concerning this flock it is that our Lord and Saviour hath promised: 'I give unto them eternal life, and they shall never perish, neither shall any pluck them out of My hands.' They who are of this society have such marks and notes of distinction from all others as are not known to our sense; only unto God, who seeth their hearts, and understandeth all their secret thoughts and cogitations; unto Him they are clear and manifest. . . . And as those everlasting promises of love, mercy, and blessedness belong to the mystical Church, even so on the other side, when we read of any duty which the Church of God is bound into, the Church whom this doth concern is a company that can be seen and known. . . . And this visible Church in like sort is but one . . . the unity of which visible body and Church of Christ consisteth of that uniformity which all several persons thereunto belonging have, by reason of that one Lord, whose servants they all profess themselves; that one faith which they all acknowledge; that one baptism wherewith they are all initiated. . . . Christians by external profession they are all, whose mark of recognisance hath in it those things (one Lord, one faith, one baptism) which we have mentioned, yea, although they be impious idolaters, wicked heretics, persons excommunicable, yea, and cast out for notorious improbity. . . . Is it then possible that the selfsame men should belong both to the synagogue of Satan and to the Church of Christ? Unto that Church which is His mystical body not possible; because that body consisteth of none but only true servants and saints of God; howbeit, of the visible body and Church of Jesus Christ those may be, and oftentimes are, in respect of the main parts of their outward profession. . . . For lack of diligent observing the difference, first between the Church of God, mystical and visible, then between the visible sound and corrupted, sometimes more, sometimes less; the oversights are neither few nor light that have been committed."[1] My brothers, that is the doctrine of Hooker, and of the Fathers, no less true than it is beautiful, on the visible as distinct from the invisible Church. To the visible Church all Christians belong who profess the one Lord, one faith, one baptism; but some more perfectly, others less completely. If heretics and men of evil life can belong to the visible Church, much more those who are neither heretics nor unrighteous, but who are altogether orthodox in the main essentials of the faith, and chiefly differ from us through the unhappy legacy of the past in divergent schemes of Church government.

We may learn much from the history of the Donatist schism in the early part of the fourth century, in the time of the Emperor Constantine. The Donatists were followers of Donatus, Bishop of Carthage, and they

[1] Hooker, *Eccl. Pol.*, iii. 1.

only differed from the rest of Christendom in their harsh treatment of those who had been weak in times of persecution. They became the dominant party in North Africa, had at one time as many as four hundred Bishops, and completely withdrew from all communion with the rest of the Churches. It was a real, determined schism. Yet Optatus, one of the Catholic writers, tells them that they were divided from the Church in part, not in every respect; for that was the nature of a schism, to be divided in part, not totally cut asunder. "Both you and we," he says, "have the same ecclesiastical conversation, the same common lessons, the same belief, the same sacraments of faith, the same mysteries. [He frequently insists to them that they were their brethren still, whether they would or not.] Though the Donatists hate us," he says, "and abhor us, and will not be called our brethren, yet we cannot depart from the fear of God; they are without doubt our brethren, though not good brethren. Therefore let no one wonder that I call them brethren, who cannot be otherwise than our brethren, seeing both they and we have one and the same spiritual nativity, though our actions are different from one another."[1]

And St. Augustine[2] always speaks in the same manner about this union in part: "In many things ye are one

[1] Optatus, lib. iii.. p. 78 (edit. Paris, 1679); iv. p. 88; v. p. 99, &c.
[2] Augustine, Epist. xlviii. ad Vincent., p. 71; in Psalm xxxii.; Conc. ii. p. 91 (tom. viii., Opp., p. 225, ed. Basil, 1569); Bingham, "Antiquities," bk. xvi. chap. i.

with us, in baptism, in the creed, and the rest of God's sacraments." And so St. Augustine, like Optatus, concludes that, whether they would or no, the Donatists were their brethren, and could not cease to be so, as long as they continued to say, " Our Father," and did not renounce their creed and their baptism. For there was no third term between Christians and pagans. If they retained faith, baptism, and the common prayer of the Lord, which teaches all men to style God their Father, so far they were Christian; and as far as they were Christians, so far were they brethren. The study of the history of the Church of Christ is always full of advantage to us, and this language to the Donatists appears to me to be very much to the purpose.

I have said that amongst other differences the main question which separates ourselves from the other Orthodox Reformed Christians of our country is that of Church government. None can fairly accuse them of wilful schism, because they are only loyal to the tradition which they have received from their fathers. Let none doubt for a moment that the external organisation of the Church is a matter of high and sacred importance. It is most desirable that we should follow as closely as possible the system of the Apostles. It is of the utmost consequence that we should hold together as far as we possibly can with the main body of Christians. I do not ask you for one single moment to alter the views which you have formed as to the historical continuity of our National Church with the Church of our primitive days. There is nobody who could set a higher value on that continuity than myself. But I may ask you, without offence, to consider in what sense this most important matter has been held by some of the greatest of our teachers.

Amongst our own authorities, Bishop Jewel[1] dwells on the essential oneness of presbyter and bishop, and maintains that, even were the continuity of English episcopal succession broken (as the Romanists declared) it could be restored from within. Archbishop Whitgift[2] met the claims of the Presbyterians for Divine right in their system not by a counter-claim for episcopacy, but by the assertion that no one certain and perfect form of government is prescribed in Scripture to the Church of Christ; and that the essential notes of the Church are only the true preaching of the Word of God, and the right administration of the Sacraments. Archbishop Bancroft,[3] a zealous High Churchman, at a conference of bishops before the consecration in St. Paul's Cathedral to Scottish sees of certain clergymen in Presbyterian orders, met an objection of Bishop Andrewes by maintaining that there was no necessity for their re-ordination, seeing, where bishops could not be had, ordination by presbyters must be deemed lawful; and in this Bishop Andrewes con-

[1] Jewel, "Defence of Apology," II. ix., § 1; v. § 1.
[2] Defence of Answer.
[3] Abp. Spottiswoode's "History," iii. 209, ed. 1851.

curred. The celebrated Bishop Hall,[1] Laud's chosen defender of episcopacy, asked men to observe the distinction which he made between the being and wellbeing of a Church, affirming that those Churches to whom the power and faculty of episcopacy is denied lose nothing of the true essence of a Church, though they lose something of their glory and perfection. The great Bishop Andrewes[2] himself, the very model of a saintly English prelate, writes—"Though our government be by Divine right, it follows not either that there is no salvation, or that a Church cannot stand, without it. He must needs be stone-blind that sees not Churches standing without it; he must needs be made of iron . . . that denies them salvation." Bishop Cosin,[3] the typical and familiar standard-bearer of High Church traditions, when in exile at Charenton in France, attended the Huguenot Sacrament, and wrote thus to a friend who had scruples on the point: "Considering there is no prohibition of our Church against it (as there is against our communicating with the Papists, and that well-grounded upon the Scripture and will of God), I do not see but that you . . . may (either in case of necessity . . . or in regard of declaring your unity in professing the same religion . . .) go otherwhiles to communicate reverently with them of

---

[1] Hall, "Defence of Remonstrance," § 14; *cf.* "Peacemaker," § 6.

[2] Andrewes, Letter II.

[3] Cosin, "Works," Anglo-Catholic Library, iv. 407; *cf.* his "Last Will," ibid. i. xxxii.

the French (Reformed) Church." The view of Archbishop Laud has already been quoted on page 104. And Hooker says—

"There may be sometimes very just and sufficient reason to allow ordination made without a bishop. The whole Church visible being the true original subject of all power, it hath not ordinarily allowed any other than bishops alone to ordain; howbeit, as the ordinary course is ordinarily in all things to be observed, so it may be in some cases not unnecessary that we decline from those ordinary ways. . . . And, therefore, we are not simply without exception to urge a lineal descent of power from the Apostles by continual succession of bishops in every effectual ordination."[1]

I have given you the opinions of these, the greatest of our Anglo-Catholic divines: Archbishop Laud, Bishop Cosin, Bishop Andrewes, Bishop Hall, Archbishop Bancroft, Bishop Jewel, and Hooker, though certainly it is not the opinion of Bellarmine the Jesuit, not because I want you to undervalue episcopacy, but because I earnestly pray that you may be able to look with a kindly and understanding eye on those whom a tradition, no less dear to them than your own is to yourselves, has led to look at this question from a very different point of view. I want you to insist, as St. Augustine insisted with the Donatists, that they are your brothers in

[1] Hooker, *Eccl. Pol.*, vii. 14.

Christ. Without abating one jot of your own legitimate convictions, I want you to follow, more than ever before, the impressive command of St. Peter: "Be ye all of one mind, having compassion one of another; love as brethren, be pitiful, be courteous; not rendering evil for evil, . . . but contrariwise blessing."

Nothing can be plainer, from the history of our own and all other Churches, than the absolute, total, and grievous failure of the policy of exasperation or persecution or unfriendliness. If we want to make our fellow-Christians more our allies and less our opponents, can anything be conceived more senseless, more ridiculous, or more disastrous than holding them at arm's length, and saying, "I can have nothing to do with you"? That was the fatal, calamitous policy in the past, which has been just the very thing that has made those who disagree from us increase in numbers and strength and in dislike of the National Church. I can imagine nothing more exquisitely calculated to confirm them in their bad opinion of ourselves than treatment so ignorant, so cruel, so un-Christian. Yet it is actually heartrending to find that such is the kind of policy which some Christian men and women think proper to pursue towards those whom we all wish to conciliate, whose opposition we desire by our gentleness and wisdom to disarm, and whose strong, honest, godly hearts we wish to win over to the great body of historical Christianity in this country. Is it not even more than unwise and senseless? Is it not disloyal and traitorous to the Church of which we are members, because it is contrary to the teaching and commands of our Lord Himself? The Jews were proud in the same manner of their spiritual pedigree and of their unimpeachable standpoint; and what was the message which John Baptist was inspired to deliver to them? "Think not to say within yourselves, We have Abraham to our father; for I say unto you that God is able of these stones to raise up children unto Abraham."[1] Nobody could have been closer to our Lord than His own mother and brethren; but He cast all other ties to the winds in comparison to a holy life: "Whosoever shall do the will of God, the same is My brother and sister and mother."[2] There was a time when John, the Apostle of Love, said, "Master, we saw one casting out devils in Thy name, and we forbade him, because he followeth not us. And Jesus said unto him, Forbid him not, for he that is not against us is on our part."[3] You cannot attempt to put a greater limitation on Christ's Presence than was placed upon it by the Lord Himself: "Where two or three are gathered together in My Name there am I in the midst of them."[4] Where Christ is welcomed as a Friend, there, surely, we may follow. "If it be possible," urged St. Paul, "as much as lieth in you live peaceably with all men."[5] On that exhortation he lays the greatest stress of which he

[1] Matt. iii. 9.   [2] Matt. xii. 50.   [3] Mark ix. 38.
[4] Matt. xviii. 20.   [5] Rom. xii. 18.

is capable. It applies to our dealings even with those who are not Christian. With what infinitely stronger cogency does it rule our conduct towards those in whose company we hope to tread the golden courts of the City of God!

It is important to remember how small are the differences which divide us from the great bodies of the Orthodox Nonconforming Christians of England compared with our bonds of Union in one faith, one Lord, one baptism, in the face of the gathering clouds of infidelity, secularism, atheism, ignorance, sin, and vice. What are questions of Church government, however important in themselves, at their own place, at their own time, compared to the evidences of a holy life, and the indwelling of the Spirit of God? Shall we not follow great examples, and each endeavour to see what we can do to conciliate our Christian fellow-subjects, and prove to them that we gladly recognise them as followers of the same Saviour, called by the same name. The best possible defence that we as Christians can offer for those venerable and priceless institutions—which we value, not for their privileges, but for their opportunities of work for the Lord—is to follow the wise and Christian precept, "In honour preferring one another." Far from uselessly trying to keep our Nonconforming brethren in the background, it should be our delight to take every opportunity of sharing our work with them, and of showing them respect and attention.

They have now little grievance except that which is purely social. It is our duty as Christians, it is our privilege as members of the National Church, and it should be our pride as patriotic citizens of the Kingdom of Christ, to remove any grounds which there may be for this last remaining complaint. From time to time we hear of unhappy and unworthy instances of arrogance, coldness, disdain, and presumption. The leading Methodists declare that the position of their body towards the National Church has been greatly altered by the intolerance of too many of the new school of young presbyters in the country villages. That is the sad old policy for exasperation; and if that policy is still pursued, who can wonder if the consequences are hostility? Why should such people expect the Nonconformists to be so much more Christian in their forbearance than themselves? How deplorable it would be if, when any humble and true servants of God are singing the words of that pathetic psalm of the Captivity, "Have mercy upon us, O Lord, have mercy upon us; for we are exceedingly filled with contempt. Our soul is exceedingly filled with the scorning of those that are at ease, and with the contempt of the proud,"—[1] it should be of us that they would be thinking! Nothing is, in truth, more touching than the friendly gratitude with which acts of kindliness and courtesy, performed in the spirit of St. Peter, are always

[1] Ps. cxxiii. 3.

welcomed by the Nonconformists. It puts us to shame, because, evidently the courtesy is not so general and customary as to be, in the way we might have hoped, a matter of course. If we desire in these days to add to the stability and to the genuine Christian character of that great institution to which we are heart and soul devoted, and to increase the Kingdom of Christ among men, then we shall, each of us, resolve to search out those of our neighbours who have hitherto been ranged in a different part of the field, and we shall unite ourselves to them by friendliness, and esteem, and affection, and honour. So shall we be helping to realise that prayer in which we join every time when we gather round the Table of the Lord, "Grant, that all they that do confess Thy holy Name may agree in the truth of Thy holy Word, and live in unity, and godly love."

VIII.

SCHISM.

"I beseech you, brethren, by the name of our Lord Jesus Christ, that there be no divisions among you; but that ye be perfectly joined together in the same mind and in the same judgment"—1 COR. i. 10.

IT would be well, I think, if we should ask the Holy Spirit of God to enable us to make some attempt to clear up our minds as to the meaning and use of the word "schism."

What St. Paul intended by it is very simple. It was the indulgence of party spirit to the verge of forming divisions. He had gone away from Corinth with his disciples Aquila and Priscilla. Aquila and Priscilla he left at Ephesus, and he himself proceeded to Jerusalem, and thence through Galatia and Phrygia. While he was traversing these countries, there was a new arrival at Corinth. Aquila and Priscilla had, at Ephesus, made acquaintance with Apollos, an eloquent and fervid Jew of Alexandria, who had hitherto been merely a disciple of John the Baptist. Under Aquila and Priscilla, Apollos completed his Christian training at Ephesus, and became a Pauline

Christian. At Corinth he stood forth as a preacher. He preached, indeed, no other than Pauline Christianity, but he presented it in a different form. He had the art of Alexandrian eloquence, and the ingenuity of Alexandrian speculation; he varied considerably from the simple manner of the Apostle; and it is probable that he entered farther than St. Paul had gone into several of the more subtle doctrines of Christianity. It is very important to note that this rift was certainly not based on any divergence in doctrine. Yet, from the variety of individual tendencies among the Corinthians, and from the personal respect and love with which men clung to the old or the new teacher respectively, the rift came to have this hurtful result. Amidst mutual jealousy some assigned the higher place to Paul and some to Apollos. It gradually came to be a point of partisanship with them to call themselves adherents of the one or the other. From the pride and irritation thus engendered, mischief and prejudice followed to the two teachers themselves, and to the Body of Christ.[1]

The matter did not end with this division into two parties. Apollos returned to Ephesus; and there arrived at Corinth Judaising Christians, provided with letters of recommendation, foolishly labouring to lower the authority of St. Paul, into whose field of work they intruded, and to exalt the authority of St. Peter. It is plain, from the whole of the First Epistle to the Corin-

---

[1] *Cf.* Meyer's "Commentary," i. 10.

thians, that they did not put forward any opposition to St. Paul's doctrine; but with their Judaising tendencies generally, with their legal prejudice as to restrictions about meats, with their stringency as to the provisions of the law, it was natural that they found acceptance with that part of the Christian community who had been Jews, for they insisted strongly on their national prerogatives.

This addition of a third party in favour of St. Peter to the two which already existed in favour of St. Paul and of Apollos, aroused a deeper feeling of the need for wholly disregarding the authority of men, which had brought about all this division into parties, and had worked for its perpetuation, and for returning to Him alone who is the Master of all, the Lord Jesus Christ.

"We belong to Christ" became accordingly a fourth watchword. Unhappily it was not the cry of all. Unhappily it was not used in its right sense and application. Unhappily it was adopted by a section only. In itself it was right; but it should have been combined with the recognition of the human instruments of Christ, St. Paul, Apollos, St. Peter. Unhappily the new party did not themselves keep clear of schismatic proceedings. They ought to have acknowledged all as, like themselves, disciples of Christ. But they organised their little array in such a manner that in their professed sanctity and lofty abstinence from partisanship they became themselves a party. Instead of including the whole community, without prejudice to the estimation due to such servants of Christ as St. Paul, Apollos, and St. Peter, in their ideal they excluded the party of St. Paul, the party of Apollos, the party of St. Peter. Think how grievously would these schisms have been aggravated if it had been in the days of newspapers! Conceive how the followers of Paul would have gloated over the *Peter Review;* how the faction of Peter would have shaken their sides over the sallies of the *Paul Banner;* how the adherents of Apollos would have swelled with satisfaction at the smart virulence of the *Apollos Times!* They still indeed assembled in one place; but they were in this fourfold division when St. Paul wrote to them this first epistle: "*I beseech you, brethren, by the name of our Lord Jesus Christ, that there be no schisms amongst you; but that ye be perfectly joined together in the same mind, and in the same judgment.*" It is comforting to us to know that when, not many years later, Clement of Rome wrote his epistle to the Church of Corinth, the wise and self-forgetful counsels of St. Paul had so far prevailed that these dissensions had not been of long continuance. Clement speaks of them as something long past and gone, with which he compares later quarrels as something worse. To St. Paul, there can then be no question that schism meant the indulgence of party spirit to the verge of forming divisions.

When we come to the days of the early Church, after the death of all the Apostles, we find schism something more definite. Schism has become the breaking off from communion with the Church, on account of disagreement in matters of faith or discipline. In this sense there must be two parties to a schism, the people who break off, and those from whom they become separated. Both may be at fault. But there were no longer inspired Apostles to warn the main body against unwise tendencies; and consequently the main body was always able to impute the blame to those who broke away. If there had always been the wisdom of St. Paul at hand, there might have been no separation. Schism might have continued a tendency rather than a definite act.

But here it is of supremest importance to remember that in these early days there were different degrees of unity and schism, according to the proportion of which a man was said to be more or less united to the main body, more or less divided from its ranks. We read in Bingham's "Ecclesiastical Antiquities"[1] how, to give a man the denomination of a true Catholic Christian, in an absolute sense, it was necessary that he should in all respects and in every kind of unity be in perfect and full communion with the Church; whereas to denominate a man a schismatic it was sufficient to break the unity of the Church in any one respect, though the gravity of the schism was to

[1] Vol. v. p. 431.

be interpreted more or less according to the degrees of separation he made from the main body—so freely and loosely was the word schismatic used in the third and fourth centuries. And as the rulers of the Church made a distinction between the degrees of schism, so did they between the censures inflicted on schismatics; for these were proportioned to the quality of the offence. It is somewhat startling to us in these days of liberty of the individual conscience to read of the strictness and severity of the discipline of the third and fourth centuries. Those who absented themselves from Church for a short time, probably a period of three weeks, were schismatics. This was the lowest degree of separation, and was punished with a few weeks' suspension of Church membership. Those who attended only some part of the service, and voluntarily withdrew from participation in Communion, were schismatics. In those days all Christians communicated. These non-communicants, who were considered schismatics in a more serious sense than those who did not go to church, were excluded for some time from all the sacred offices of religion. The third sort of separatists were those who withdrew totally from intercourse with the main body, and justified their separation. Yet even heretics, excommunicate persons, and profane men were considered in some sense of the Church, as having received baptism, which they always retained, and as making profession of some part of the Christian faith; but because in other respects they were broken off from her, they were not esteemed sound and perfect members of the body. This distinction between total and partial unity, and total and partial schism and separation, is of great use, says this learned and impartial authority, to make us understand all those sayings of the ancients which speak of heretics and schismatics, and even excommunicate persons and profligate sinners, as being in some measure in and out of the Church.

It is very desirable that we should notice how St. Jerome, speaking of schism, seems to identify its development with heresy; in his opinion, apparently, a separation which did not involve heretical doctrine would be less serious. "Schism, at the beginning," he says, "may be understood to be something different from heresy; but there is no schism which does not invent some heresy for itself, in order to justify its secession." Now we must remember that in the unfortunate and unavoidable divisions of modern Christendom there is in many cases no heretical doctrine at all.

In the ages before the Reformation there were even more momentous schisms than those which have since occurred. In the fourth century there was the separation of the followers of Donatus, which involved 400 Bishops and a great part of the flourishing Church of North Africa, until it was swept away by the invasion of the Goths. Others, which inundated large tracts of Christendom, were the separations of the heretical churches of the Arians, Photinians, and Apollinarians. There was a great schism in the illustrious Church of Antioch, caused by Lucifer, a Sardinian bishop. In the fifth century there was the notable schism in the orderly Church of Rome between Laurentius and Symmachus. In the ninth century came the tremendous rent between East and West, between Constantinople and Rome, which has lasted ever since. In the fourteenth century Europe was deluged with blood, because of the schism between the rival popes of Rome and Avignon, which lasted till the end of the Council of Pisa, in 1409.

In the thirteenth century we come to an authoritative definition of schism, which is totally unlike those which we have already considered. It lands us altogether in a new stage of thought. It points to the real cause of all the subsequent splits and troubles. The great doctor of the Western Church in the thirteenth century was St. Thomas Aquinas. "Schismatics," says St. Thomas Aquinas, "are those who of their own will and intention sever themselves from the unity of the Church." This unity of the Church, he continues, consists of the connection of its members with each other, and of all the members with the Head. "Now, this Head is Christ, whose representative in the Church is the Supreme Pontiff. And, therefore, the name of schismatics is given to those who refuse to be under the Supreme Pontiff, and to communicate with the members of the Church subject to him." It was this intolerable and unchristian doctrine, with all its accompaniments of error, which was the cause of that Reformation which, in the sixteenth century, blazed suddenly forth at once in all the countries of Northern Europe.

My brothers, our English Church was indeed favoured by God in being able to retain its ancient historical link of outward organisation with the Church of the Apostles, and at the same time to purify its doctrine in accordance with the standard of the Word of God. It is true that to by far the largest and most ancient body in Christendom we are excommunicated schismatics: the 190 millions of the Church of Rome will not allow us even to be a church at all. It is true that they are openly boasting that our poor little feeble Church is rapidly moving towards them, and will soon be swallowed up by their vast and orderly hosts. It is true that we were obliged to break off from the Patriarchate of the West, which originally sent the mission of St. Augustine to the Saxons, and which we had always acknowledged as it was acknowledged by the Gallican Church of France. It is true that we once stood in much the same relation to the Church of Rome in which the Episcopal Church of America or the Church of South Africa stands to the Church of England. It is true that we were compelled to separate from that Patriarchate because we could no longer hold the Supremacy of the Pope, the Doctrine of the Corporal Presence, the Sacrifice of the Mass, the Worship of the Virgin, the Worship of Saints, the Worship of Images, the Worship of Relics, the Doctrine of Purgatory, the Doctrine of Compulsory Confession and Absolution, the Denial of the Cup to the Laity, the compulsory Celibacy of the Clergy, Works of Supererogation, the equal authority of Tradition with Scripture, and the Superiority of the Monastic Life. It is true that to the eighty-four millions of the Greek Church we, twenty-three millions of English-speaking Episcopalians, are Separatists, because we were once part of the Western Patriarchate, and with them added a clause to the Creed known now as the Nicene. It is true that we are not on terms of full Communion with the Reformed Churches of Switzerland, Germany, France, Holland, Denmark, Sweden, Norway, and Scotland, because they have either an incomplete Episcopalian government, or a different form of organisation. But, holding to the Apostolic faith and the Apostolic order in a good conscience, we can bear with patience the name of schismatics, even from those 190 millions, who form probably the majority of Christendom. We remember the wise and beautiful words of the present Bishop of Durham: "There never was an epoch since the Church spread beyond Jerusalem when the 'one body of Christ' was one in visible uniformity, or even one in perfect sympathy. Time has, indeed, hardened and multiplied the difference between the several parts into which the Church is divided but it is possible to trace already in the Apostolic age the essential features of those divisions over which we grieve. And if we look forward to the great promise which gladdens the future, it is not that there shall ever be, as we wrongly read, 'one fold,' one outward society of Christians gathered in one outward form, but what answers more truly to present experience and reasonable hope, 'one flock and one Shepherd.' And in the meantime, let us rate the differences of Christians as highly as we will, there yet remains a common faith, in the presence of which they are almost as nothing. He who believes, to take the ground of the Apostolic message on the day of Pentecost, that Christ rose from the dead; he who is baptized into Him; he who rejoices, though trembling, in the pledge of a glorified humanity, is divided from the world without by an interval as wide as that between life and death. In this one faith, one baptism, one hope of our calling, lies a universal fellowship of believers, the symbol and the earnest of the brotherhood of men, the single truths, which taken alone, distinguishes for ever Christian from ancient thought."[1]

My brothers, I said it was of the supremest importance to remember that in the earlier days, when there was yet a visible unity, there were different degrees both of unity and schism, according to the proportion of which a man was said to be more or less united to the main body, or divided from its ranks. Degrees in schism; some necessary, some venial, some more

[1] Bishop Westcott on the Creed.

serious—that is the point for us to recollect. At the present moment there is no Church which is not in schism or division with some other Church: the Roman from the Greek, the English from the Roman, the non-Episcopalians from those who have the episcopal order. Here comes in the principle of difference in degree of schism. Take, for instance, ourselves. We, by God's mercy, and the wisdom of Queen Elizabeth, were able to recover our episcopal order. The reformers of Switzerland, Germany, France, Scandinavia, and Poland, from whom all other Protestant bodies have sprung, wished to retain episcopal government, but could not persuade their Bishops to join them. The Augsburg Confession, the basis of the faith of the Reformed Church of Germany, says, with a touching pathos, "We would willingly preserve the ecclesiastical and canonical government, if the Bishops would only cease to exercise cruelty upon our churches."[1] Melanchthon wrote to Luther:[2] "I know not with what face we can refuse bishops if they will suffer us to have purity of doctrine." In another place Melanchthon says, "Luther did always judge as I do." Calvin wrote:[3] "Bishops have invented no other form of governing the Church but such as the Lord hath prescribed by His own word." After describing the character of a truly Christian bishop, he adds with great solemnity, "I should account

[1] See Bishop Hall's "Episcopacy by Divine Right," p. 11.
[2] Brett's "Church Government," p. 121.
[3] Calvin, *Epist. ad Martin Schaling* and *Tract. de Reform. Eccles.*

those men deserving of envy, the severest anathema, who do not submit themselves reverently and with all obedience to such a hierarchy." Bucer wrote:[1] "We see by the constant practice of the Church, even from the time of the Apostles, how it hath pleased the Holy Ghost, that among the ministers to whom the government of the Church is especially committed, one individual should have the chief management of the churches and of the whole ministry, and should in that management take precedence of all his brethren. For which reason the title of Bishop is employed to designate a chief spiritual governor." Beza always warmly commended the English Church polity.[2] "If," said he, with vehement stress, "there be any who altogether reject episcopal jurisdiction (a thing I can hardly be persuaded of), God forbid that any one in his senses should give way to the madness of such men." I could quote similar opinions from the Reformers of Poland,[3] Hungary, Italy, Norway, Sweden, and Scotland;[4] from Grotius,[5] and from the Synod of Dort in

[1] Bucer, *De Regno Christi.*
[2] Brett on Church Government, v. 85; Durel, "View of the Reformed Churches," 4to, 1662, p. 280; Theod. Beza, *Ad Tract. de Minist.*
[3] *Canon. Eccl. Synod. Corniathinæ in Hungariâ,* iii. 8; Zanchius, *De verâ Reformandarum Ecclesiarum Ratione.*
[4] Abp. Spottiswoode, *Refutatio Libelli,* A.D. 1620; Bishop Lindsay, "True Narrative," A.D. 1618; Bishop Ross, "Episcopacy not abjured in Scotland;" Bishop Sage's "Vindication," chap. iv.
[5] Grotius, *Discussio de Primatu Papæ; de Imper. Summ. Potest. circa sacra,* xi. 5.

Holland.[1] The fact is, that the original aversion of the Reformed Churches for the Episcopal form of government has been greatly exaggerated. What drove them from Episcopacy was the cruelty, wickedness, blindness, and ignorance of the Catholic Bishops abroad and in Scotland at the time of the Reformation. The attitude they were then compelled to adopt has become since then a time-honoured tradition. To talk of them as deliberately leaving the Catholic Church is to pass over the very plainest facts of history. They wished to carry on the ancient form and the ancient chain of connection just like ourselves. But they could not. They had no Queen Elizabeth, and they had no Archbishop Parker. Subsequent generations, finding that they could enjoy a spiritual life without the ancient order, became less and less inclined to share the regret and anxiety of the first Reformers. And now that which was at first regarded as an imperfect form of government has come to be looked upon as a precious heritage; and as we recognise the right of the two millions of our Roman Catholic fellow-subjects in this country to have their own organisation, we can hardly refuse that right to the conscientious and hereditary representatives of the influence of the Reformed Churches of Scotland and of the Continent. We remember the ancient principle of the primitive Church, that there are different degrees of unity and

[1] Collier, "Eccl. Hist.," ii. p. 718; Archdeacon John Sinclair's "Dissertations," 1833.

schism, according to the proportion of which a man is said to be more or less united to the Church or divided from it; and that they who retain faith and baptism, and the common form of Christian worship, are in those respects at unity with the Church; though in other respects, in which their schism or division consists, they may be divided from her.

But at the same time we long, with an earnestness which nothing can abate, that they would come back to the main body of Christianity in this country. Our bishops are not the prelatical tyrants that they are sometimes described, but very like the presidents of the early Church—first amongst equals. Would that those who are not against us, though they are not outwardly of us, could see the advantage of following the opinions of the early Reformers in joining once more with that simple and universal type of government! Would that they could feel with Richard Baxter that divisions are the killing of the Church, or the wounding of it at least; that they are its deformities; that they are not only our own dishonour, but the injurious dishonour of Christ, and of religion, and of the Gospel; that they lamentably hinder the progress of the Gospel and the conversion and salvation of the ungodly world; that they lay open the Churches of Christ, not only to the scorn, but to the malice, will, and fury of their enemies; that they greatly hinder the edification of the members of the Church, while they are possessed with envyings and dislike one of another! Would that they could see that, so long as we agree with the main body in essentials, it is not necessary to break off, in consequence of any little disagreement, from all the little particular unessential points which have inevitably grown round the original system in the changes and chances of a long and varying history!

But, my brothers, it is, lastly, imperatively urgent that each one of ourselves should, to the very utmost of our power, discourage the schismatic spirit in ourselves and others within our Church itself. Lord Bacon, in his immortal essay on "Unity in Religion," told us how men ought to take heed of rending God's Church by two kinds of controversies: the one is, when the matter of the point controverted is too small and light, nor worth the heat and strife about it, kindled only by contradiction; for, as it is noted by one of the Fathers, Christ's coat indeed had no seam, but the Church's vesture was of divers colours; whereupon he said, "Let there be variety in the robe, but let there be no rent; they be two things, unity and uniformity. The other is, when the matter of the point is great, but it is driven to an overgreat subtilty and obscurity, so that it becometh a thing rather ingenious than substantial. A man that is of judgment and understanding shall sometimes hear ignorant men differ, and know well within himself that those which so differ mean one thing, and yet they themselves would never agree; and if it come so to pass in that distance of judgment which is between man and man, shall we not think that God above, that knows the heart, doth not discern that frail men, in some of their contradictions, mean the same thing, and accepteth of both? Men create oppositions which are not, and put them into new terms so fixed; so that, whereas the meaning ought to govern the term, the term in effect governeth the meaning."

Preaching at St. Paul's Cathedral forty-seven years ago, at Bishop Blomfield's Visitation, a former Archdeacon of Middlesex[1] said, "In our own Church the same carnal or sectarian humour (which was amongst the Corinthians) has in a greater or less degree at all times betrayed itself. It could hardly be expected that this evidence of the corruption and infirmity of human nature should in our case be wanting; and accordingly notwithstanding all our helps to unity, and all our daily prayers for this blessing to the Divine 'author of peace and lover of concord,' we have always lamentably suffered from religious factions and divisions. The terms High Church and Low Church, Puritan and Cavalier, Orthodox and Evangelical, Arminian and Calvinist, are no sooner pronounced than they suggest to many minds antagonist associations of bitterness and dislike." My brothers, can we say that we are better now than our fathers were forty-seven years ago? Is not this the true schismatical spirit in the Apostolical sense? "I am of Paul, and I of Apollos, and I of

[1] Archdeacon John Sinclair.

Peter, and I of Christ." That was what St. Paul complained of. Is it not the same? "I am of Newman, and I of Pusey, and I of Maurice, and I of Wesley, and I of Calvin, and I of Luther? I am of the vestments, I am of the coloured stoles, I am of the black gown, I am of the cope and mitre, I am of the Roman collar, I am of the lighted tapers, I am of the incense, I am of the crucifix, I am of the eastward position, I am of the kneeling at the Epistle, I am of the divided words of administration, I am of the use of Sarum, I am of the First Prayer-book, I am of the English Church Union, I am of the Confraternity of the Blessed Sacrament, I am of this Society or that? My brothers, are ye not carnal? Is Christ divided? These things are harmless and immaterial in themselves, but when pursued factiously and as matters of importance, they are schismatic. How, if some great storm of misguided secularistic fury were to burst upon her, would our Church stand in that evil day if we are so imbued with the schismatic spirit? Oh, my brothers, by the love you bear to your Saviour, by the loyalty which you owe to the English Church, I implore you to cease to exaggerate trifles, to give up banding yourselves together for the propagation of particular phases of doctrine, to look in all things to the Word of God for the estimation of the relative importance of controversies! I urge you to disband these associations, to shake off the trammels of these personal traditions, and to go back in all things to the simplicity that is in

Christ! The nearer we are to Him, the nearer we shall be to each other. Human authority, human influence, may be recognised in its proper place; but when it divides us into parties, and distorts great truths, and destroys proportions, and fills us with the fierce glee of sectarian fury, then certainly it is not of God. I entreat you to depart from these positions and associations, which might in different times be tolerable, but which are now of necessity deeply imbued with the evil spirit of division. "I *beseech* you, brethren, by the name of our Lord Jesus Christ, that there be no schisms among you; but that ye be perfectly joined together in the same mind and in the same judgment!"

IX.

CURRENT FALLACIES IN THE CHURCH.

"I firmly believe the influence of your personal ministry does more than the labours of an open enemy to wean from the pure faith and simple ritual of our Church the affections of many amongst her children. . . . You seem to me to be habitually assuming the place and doing the work of a Roman confessor, and not that of an English clergyman."—Bishop SAMUEL WILBERFORCE to Dr. PUSEY.

THERE are certain fallacies by which we are in the present day beset, and about which it would be well for all true adherents of Reformation principles to be perfectly clear in their own minds.

The first is that there were doctrines not taught by Christ, and unknown by the Apostles before the Day of Pentecost, which were to be disclosed by the Holy Spirit. The maintainers of this fallacy are much given to quoting the words of St. John xvi. 13: "When He, the Spirit of truth, is come, He will guide you into all truth." They do not go on, however, to quote the rest of the utterance in the words which immediately succeed, and which would at once set them right. They are these: "For He shall not speak of Himself; but whatsoever He shall hear, that shall

He speak; and He will show you things to come. He shall glorify Me; for He shall receive of Mine, and shall show it unto you." The idea that the Holy Spirit would produce anything not taught by Christ is most perverse. It is entirely precluded by these words. If any additional light on our Lord's meaning is needed, it may be found in the parallel passage in chapter xiv. ver. 26: "But the Comforter, which is the Holy Ghost, Whom the Father will send in My name, He shall teach you all things, and bring all things to your remembrance, whatsoever I have said unto you." As Luther said: "He imposeth a limit and measure to the preaching of the Holy Ghost Himself; He is to preach nothing new, nothing other than Christ and His Word—to the end that we might have a sure sign, a certain test, whereby to judge false spirits." Thus the Spirit is conditioned by the Son, as the Son is by the Father. More than once we are told that the disciples needed interpretation of our Lord's words: "They understood not that saying, and were afraid to ask Him."[1] "They understood not the saying which He spake unto them."[2] "They understood not that He spake unto them of the Father."[3] "This parable spake Jesus unto them; but they understood not what things they were which He spake unto them."[4] "They understood none of these things; and this saying was hid from them, neither knew they

---

[1] Mark ix. 32.
[2] Luke ii. 50.
[3] John viii. 27.
[4] John x. 6.

the things which were spoken."[1] "These things understood not His disciples at the first, but when Jesus was glorified then remembered they that these things were written of Him, and that they had done these things unto Him."[2] The office of the Spirit was to be that of an interpreter. He was to bring the innumerable words of our Lord back to the minds of His disciples; He was to interpret them, show their ground in the Old Testament, and their application to their existing circumstances. But in the most important period of the manifestation of the Holy Spirit, from Pentecost to Revelation, there is not one single trace of any shred of teaching different from the teaching of our Lord. It is the law of Christ that the Christians are to obey.[3] It is the word of Christ which is to dwell in them richly.[4] It is the Word of the truth of the Gospel that they have heard.[5] The Word is something already known—they are to preach it in season and out of season. A bishop is to hold fast the faithful word as he hath been taught.[6] Our Church is abundantly apostolical in this point, when we are taught that "Holy Scripture containeth all things necessary to salvation: so that whatsoever is not read therein, nor may be proved thereby, is not to be required of any man that it should be believed as an article of the faith, or be thought requisite or necessary

---

[1] Luke xviii. 34. [2] John xii. 16.
[3] Gal. vi. 2. [4] Col. iii. 16.
[5] Col. i. 5. [6] Tit. i. 9.

to salvation."[1] The Apostles taught nothing that Christ did not teach; the Church can teach nothing but what was taught by the Apostles and by Christ.

The second fallacy is that during the forty days after the resurrection our Lord communicated to the Apostles a number of new doctrines which do not appear in the Gospels, Acts, or Epistles. This fallacy is grounded on the simple words at the beginning of the Acts of the Apostles: "The former treatise have I made, O Theophilus, of all the things that Jesus began both to do and teach, until the day in which He was taken up, after that He through the Holy Ghost had given commandments unto the Apostles whom He had chosen: to whom also He showed Himself alive after His passion by many infallible proofs, being seen of them forty days, and speaking of the things pertaining to the kingdom of God."[2] Never was tremendous inference laid on less solid foundation. The point here is that all that Jesus did and taught till His ascension St. Luke has already recorded. He maintains that in all necessary particulars his account of the life of Jesus is full and complete. Of the precious words which He spoke of the things pertaining to the kingdom of God, St. Luke has already given the most important and characteristic specimen in his account of the walk to Emmaus: "Then He said unto them, O fools, and slow of heart to believe all that the prophets have spoken: ought not Christ

[1] Article VI. [2] Acts i. 1.

to have suffered these things, and to enter into His glory? And beginning at Moses and all the prophets, He expounded unto them in all the Scriptures the things concerning Himself."[1] And again in the same chapter, in his account of the interview with the Apostles, St. Luke gives another specimen of what he means: "He said unto them, These are the words which I spake unto you, while I was yet with you, that all things must be fulfilled which were written in the Law of Moses, and in the prophets, and in the psalms, concerning Me. Then opened He their understanding that they might understand the Scriptures, and said unto them: Thus it is written, and thus it behoved Christ to suffer, and to rise from the dead the third day; and that repentance and remission of sins should be preached among all nations, beginning at Jerusalem, and ye are witnesses of these things."[2] No shadow of a hint is given of new doctrine, or sacerdotal teaching, or the foundation of institutions. If there had been, the passage at the beginning of the Acts would have been the very place in which St. Luke would sketch them. No hint of such a thing is given in St. Matthew, St. Mark, or St. John. No authority of our Lord is invoked for any of the adaptations of Christian institutions to circumstances, where, had the fallacy been true, such citation would have been inevitable. Nothing is attributed to our Lord in all the Acts and Epistles

[1] Luke xxiv. 25.   [2] Luke xxiv. 44.

that is not taught in the Gospels, except some well-known phrase of His, "It is more blessed to give than to receive"[1]—words which, after all, only summarise a large portion of His recorded teaching. Nothing can be more obvious than the meaning of St. Luke. Our Lord's visits to His Apostles after His resurrection are few and far between; the chief of them are recorded by St. Paul. Had He given any new directions, these could not have failed to appear in the text of the New Testament. If once you suppose that Christ, during His brief appearances, gave instructions not recorded in His life, and not alluded to in the Epistles, you may just as easily believe that He prophesied of the invocation of saints, the worship of the Virgin, the doctrine of purgatory, indulgences, the Mass, the celibacy of the clergy, the five sacraments, auricular confession, the Virgin's Immaculate Conception, the worship of images, and the Infallibility of the Pope.

The third fallacy, which at the present day meets us, is that there were a number of matters so important and so sacred in the eyes of the Apostles, that they were afraid to mention them for fear of the Jews and pagans, or even to give any hint of them in their Epistles. It is in this way that audacious and uncritical writers explain the fact that the mentions made in the New Testament of the Lord's Supper are not so numerous or important as they would wish,

[1] Acts xx. 35.

the comparatively minor stress that is laid upon it, and the total silence about any liturgical service, or any transfer of the Aaronic vestments to the Christian presbyters. But if that was really the case, or anything more than the most gratuitous fancy, it would follow that the Lord's Supper would not be mentioned at all; whereas St. Paul gives an explicit account of its institution. It is sometimes, in the same prejudiced manner, argued that when St. Paul rebuked the Corinthians for abuses, he could not have been alluding to the Lord's Supper, but to the Love Feast. Then, why should he inextricably and fundamentally bind up his rebuke of the excesses with his account of the institution?[1] And again, the breaking of bread is constantly and frequently mentioned. This argument, that Scripture was silent about matters either too familiar for explanation or too sacred to be mentioned, will not bear an instant's examination. Scripture is not silent about them at all, but frequently mentions them, and gives them their due place and proportion. If there had been any real sacrificial teaching in connection with the Holy Communion, the Epistle to the Hebrews would have been the place of all others for such doctrine. If such doctrine had been in vogue, and yet the Epistle to the Hebrews remained silent, it would have been not merely incomplete but misleading.

[1] 1 Cor. xi. 22.

The fourth fallacy I wish to mention is connected with the word "Romish." There is an ambiguity about it which is a most disastrous and unfortunate circumstance in our present controversies. The most extreme of the innovating party declare that they are not Romanising, because there are just two points in the present condition of Rome after which they have no hankering. They do not accept the Infallibility of the Pope and the Immaculate Conception of the Virgin Mary, which are recent additions to the Romish Creed. And they lay great stress on the fact that before the Reformation the Church of England sometimes tried to declare its comparative autonomy and independence of the Romish See. But the real point is that, from the time of St. Augustine downwards to the Reformation, the Mediæval Church of England did follow the developments of the doctrines of the Church of Rome, and was as thoroughly "Romish" in her teachings and practice as any other portion of Christendom. The appeal of the Reformation, by which we of the Church of England are all bound, was most distinctly not to the time of St. Augustine, but to the authority of Holy Scripture itself, considerable importance being attributed to the witness and evidence of the first three centuries. This ambiguity, which gives occasion to assert that the doctrines of the Mediæval Church were not Romish, gives rise to this very grave fallacy, which has momentous consequences at the present day amongst the younger clergy. The Use of Sarum, to which they appeal, was not identical with the Use of Rome, but it taught the same doctrines. It is the doctrine which is of importance, not the mere phrases or varieties of ceremony by which it is expressed. The laity at large have no conception of the gravity of this fallacy. They are constantly told that things, practices, and doctrines are not Romish, because there was some variation in the national customs of the unreformed English Church. When the extreme innovators are accused of moving Romewards, they declare they are not moving to Rome, but to Sarum. They mean that they do not propose to accept the Infallibility of the Pope or the Immaculate Conception of the Virgin; and they also mean that they are not going to adopt Romish colours, or distinctively Romish ceremonies as apart from the ceremonies of Sarum. This is in reality only a quibble, although no doubt it represents some important distinction to their own minds; for the doctrines of the Church of England during the ascendancy of the Use of Sarum, towards which these men are desirous to move, were most distinctly Romish. Sarum merely means Rome minus the Infallibility of the Pope and the Immaculate Conception of the Virgin. But the protest of England against Rome was three centuries before the Infallibility of the Pope and the Immaculate Conception of the Virgin were thought of or invented. It is Rome in the guise of Sarum that we have thoroughly and once for all repudiated, and that we have once more to repel.

The fifth fallacy commonly in vogue is in the use of the word "Catholic."[1] Its true use is to distinguish the Church or Churches which hold to the simple teaching of the New Testament from those which are heretical, and which, as holding some peculiar view of their own, are not universal. As regards institutions or doctrines, its proper meaning is that which has been held always, everywhere, and by everybody. The great truths of Christianity taught by the New Testament, and the simple institutions of Bishop, Priest, Deacon, Baptism, the Lord's Supper, and the weekly meeting for Prayer, are therefore Catholic. Little else is worthy of the name. To usurp it for the mere usages, customs, and doctrines of a Church calling itself Catholic, whether they themselves have been held always, everywhere, and by everybody, or not, is an abuse of terms. It is a good, useful, and important historical word, and should be vindicated from the slavery to which it has been subjected.

Against a sixth fallacy I would ask you to protest with all your hearts and souls. It is in the application of the word "Churchman" or "good Churchman." "What sort of a Churchman is he?" is a question that is asked every day. Those who ask it generally mean that they wish the subject of their inquiry to

[1] *Cf.* Chap. iv.

be one who puts the mediæval doctrines of and about the Church above the plain and simple teaching and authority of Scripture; one who places so disproportionate a value on the outward body and its developments that he has become out of harmony with the balance of Scriptural doctrine; one who thinks more of the mediæval Church of England than of the principles of the Reformation; one who thanks God that, in spite of much that was to be deplored at the Reformation settlement, certain unexpected treasures have been handed down, the existence of which has in modern times been rediscovered. Now, in the early Church, a true Churchman was one who, while holding, of course, to the great principles of Catholic truth, obeyed the customs of his own Church, and was guided by his own bishop.[1] If a man wished without authority to copy the customs of other Churches, and disregard the example and advice of his bishop, so far he was not in harmony with Catholic principles. Much was left to be settled by the taste and feelings of individual Churches. That is a principle on which our Church has claimed full liberty. Her own principles are expressed with abundant clearness. It is those who are loyal to those principles who, according to the rules of the primitive and Catholic Church, are the true and genuine Churchmen. It is those who, under some strange mediæval hallucination, adopt the principles,

---

[1] Bingham, "Eccl. Antiq.," bk. xvi. § 10.

teachings, and customs of other Churches, which are not really Catholic, but Roman, and which our own Church has by its own inherent authority distinctly repudiated, who incur the censure of faulty and imperfect Churchmanship.

Another mistake I may be permitted to mention. It is that of taking up some name or phrase characteristic of the carnal movement, and using it in a new sense as if it were perfectly harmless. It is supposed that, by the fact that you use it yourself, you have taken all the sting out of it. You perhaps hear it said, "I am a sacerdotalist. You are sacerdotalists. We are all sacerdotalists. The sacerdotalism we all believe in is the sole priesthood of our Lord Jesus Christ." Well, of course that is very true in the sense in which it is used; but if we all go about calling ourselves sacerdotalists, in some peculiar esoteric metaphorical sense, we shall only succeed in being considered to agree with those of whom the name is really and truly characteristic. The name sacerdotalist belongs to those who insist on the sacrificial vicarious priesthood. The name Catholic, in its proper sense, belongs to us. The name Protestant belongs to us. But the name sacerdotalist is obviously misleading, and we have no excuse for meddling with it.[1]

[1] It is because the sin-offering has ceased that peace-offerings, freewill-offerings, and thank-offerings have become possible. These spiritual sacrifices took the concrete form in the early Church of an offertory, which was the life of the whole institution, and was naturally emphasised by preachers, by diptychs, and other

One more fallacy before I conclude. The use of the adjective High-church is full of ambiguity. In its application it is a very relative term. In Queen Anne's days it meant something very different from what it means now. But we must not allow its concentration upon the most extreme or ritualistic section of the Church to persuade us that against those who are not ritualistic we have no point of difference or disagreement. There are many among those who follow the divines of the seventeenth rather than of the sixteenth century who wish to persuade us that only the men who wear vestments are High-churchmen, and that they themselves are the truest members of the Church of England. Now, we do not wish to multiply differences, but at the same time we cannot consent, by any shifting of recognised historical terms, to have our minds confused and the teaching of our Church obscured. Otherwise, every succeeding generation would be going further down the scale, until the old framework of the Reformed Church of England would be left like the ark on the top of Ararat.[1]

contrivances, and still persists as the Great Entrance in the liturgies. These are real and true sacrifices, whereas the carnal, renewed sacrifice of the Body and Blood of Christ is untrue to Scripture. To stop at the sin-offering is to stop at the threshold of the Tabernacle, before the true worship has even begun. The ignorance of the Romanists and their imitators is remarkable.

[1] There is a historial High Church party in the Church of England, who are as distinct from the Ritualists as the Reformers themselves. They should be proud of their name, and not allow it to be usurped by the mediæval Counter-Reformation.

You have a glorious position to vindicate, and an unrivalled opportunity of making its establishment sure and certain. The country is waiting to hear what you, as well as the clergy, can say for your attitude and your belief. You have on your side the Bible and the Prayer-book. Of this the innovators are conscious, for they have now made definite proposals for the Prayer-book's alteration. You have on your side the great mass of quiet religious men, who dislike ritualism, the confessional, the sacrifice of the Mass, and the sacrificial priesthood. You have the Archbishop condemning disparagers of the Reformation, and declaring it to be the greatest event since the publication of Christianity. You have the Bishops pronouncing that fasting communion is not obligatory, and that evening communion is under circumstances permissible, whereas the contrary propositions have been for years earnestly taught by the mediævalists. Oh, make use of this great opportunity. Establish your Pastorate at Oxford. Build your own theological college in the provinces. Maintain Reformation principles in every assembly of laity and clergy. Prove to the Nonconformists that the Church is still what for three hundred years she has been claimed to be, the bulwark of an intelligent and truly Catholic protest against Rome. Support Reformation literature. Distribute wise and well-grounded Reformation pamphlets throughout the country. The ceaseless vigilance of Rome never slumbers; she uses the mediævalists for her own vast, far-sighted, patient, and comprehensive purposes.[1] Have the courage of your opinions. Recommend them by the earnestness, devotion, and self-sacrifice of your lives. Win the working-classes by the true brotherliness of your sympathy. And may God Himself continually shield us from pride, presumption, and error, and give us a right judgment in all things!

[1] "The very Establishment which was set up in rivalry to the Church, with a Royal supremacy triumphantly pitted against a Papal supremacy—this very Establishment has changed its temper and attitude. Its bishops, ministers, and people are busily engaged in ignoring or denouncing those very Articles which were drawn up to be their eternal protest against the old religion. The sacramental power of orders, the need of jurisdiction, the Real Presence, the daily sacrifice, auricular confession, prayers and offices for the dead, belief in purgatory, the invocation of the Blessed Virgin and the saints, religious vows, and the institution of monks and nuns —the very doctrines stamped in the Thirty-nine Articles as fond fables and blasphemous deceits—all these are now openly taught from a thousand pulpits within the Establishment, and as heartily embraced by as many crowded congregations." (Speech of Cardinal Vaughan when Bishop of Salford, July 1890.) Without adopting the language as wholly accurate (especially his statement about the bishops), we must take note of its general tone and drift.

X.

INDEPENDENCE AND RIGHTS OF NATIONAL CHURCHES.

"The necessity of polity and regiment in all Churches may be held without holding any one certain form to be necessary in them all."—HOOKER, *Eccl. Pol.*, bk. iii. chap. ii. § 1.

IN the anxiety of many excellent persons that there should be as little difference as possible between the chief branches of the Christian Church, they are in danger of forgetting to some extent the independence of different Churches one of the other, and the unimportance of uniformity, or even similarity, so long as they hold the main essentials of the Christian faith.

The origin of National Churches was even to be distinguished in the time of the Apostles, when St. Paul grouped together "the Churches of Judæa,"[1] "the Churches of Galatia,"[2] "the Churches of Macedonia."[3] Another instance of nationality is seen in the fact that the converts from Judaism were always allowed to continue the Mosaic worship, while the Gentiles were free from its regulations. It was not

[1] Acts ix. 31; Gal. i. 22. [2] 1 Cor. xvi. 1. [3] 2 Cor. viii. 1.

till the reign of the Emperor Hadrian, about 135 A.D., that the main body of Jewish Christians finally separated from the Law.

Dean Jackson points out that the Churches planted by St. Paul could not appeal to St. Peter, nor those planted by St. Peter to any other Apostle. "Admitting,"[1] he goes on, "the laws and discipline of all the Churches planted by St. Peter, by St. Paul, and other Apostles had been the selfsame, yet could they not in this respect be so truly and properly called one visible Church, as the particular Churches planted by St. Paul, especially in one and the same province, were one Church, albeit their laws or ordinances had been more different. It is probable, then, that there were as many several distinct visible Churches as there were Apostles, or other ambassadors of Christ. . . . It is, then, profession of the same faith, participation of the sacrament, and subjection to the same laws and ordinances ecclesiastic which makes the visible Church to be one. It is the diversity of independent judicature, or supreme tribunals ecclesiastic, which makes plurality of visible Churches, or distinguisheth one from the other. That which makes every visible Church to be more or less the true Church of God, is the greater or less efficacy or conformity of its public doctrine and discipline for adapting or fashioning the visible members of it that they may become live members

[1] Dean Jackson's Works, xii. chap. viii. § 5.

of the holy Catholic Church (the true invisible body of Christ), or living stones of the New Jerusalem. Every true visible Church is an inferior freehold or nursery for training up scholars that they may be fit to be admitted into the celestial academy. . . . There have been as many visible Churches independent each on other, for matter of jurisdiction or subjection to one visible head, as there be several free states or Christian kingdoms independent one of another. The subordination of Church to Church is in proportion the same with the subordination of the several states wherein the Churches are planted. The best union that can be expected between visible Churches seated in kingdoms or commonweals independent one of another, is the unity of league or friendship. And this may be as strict as it shall please such commonweals or Churches to make it. To make the Church seated in one absolute state or kingdom live in subjection to another Church seated in another kingdom, or to any member of another Church or kingdom (head or branch), is to erect a Babel, or seat of Antichrist, not to build up one holy Church to Christ. This practice of usurpation of the Romish Church hath been the reason why the Christian world for these many years hath been more confused and disordered than the synagogue of Mahomet."

When Christianity first began its systematic organisation it was all within the limits of one great empire. The Apostles had followed the civil divisions in the founding and extent of their Churches, and their followers carried out the system on the same lines. The Roman Empire was itself divided into dioceses with subordinate provinces, and the Churches obviously took their model in setting up metropolitical and patriarchal power and the union of dioceses from this plan of the State. As in every metropolis, or chief city of each province, there was a superior magistrate above the magistrates of every single city, so likewise in the same metropolis there was a bishop whose power extended over the whole province, whence he was called the Metropolitan or Primate, as being the principal bishop of the province; and in all places the see of this bishop was fixed to the civil metropolis, except in Africa, where the primatery passed from bishop to bishop, according to seniority. In the same way as the State had a Vicarius in every capital city of each civil diocese, so the Churches in process of time came to have their exarchs, or patriarchs, in many, if not in all, the capital cities of the empire.[1]

It was in consequence of the breaking up of the Roman Empire that Provincial Churches have been succeeded by National Churches.

"The external causes of the change are to be found in the history of the Teutonic kingdoms which rose upon the ruins of the Roman Empire. The limits of those kingdoms were constantly shifting, and were

[1] Bingham, "Eccl. Antiq.," bk. ix. chap. i. § 4.

determined without regard to the limits of existing dioceses or provinces. For, whereas the latter had been determined, in Roman times, chiefly by the areas of settlement of the original tribes of the Celts, the latter were determined by the areas of settlement or conquest of the intrusive tribes of the Teutons. Each kingdom found an ecclesiastical organisation existing, and endeavoured to incorporate it. The earlier bonds began to give way under the pressure of the new need of keeping the kingdom together. The king gathered together the bishops and clergy within their domain, irrespective of the earlier arrangements. The bishops and clergy obeyed the king's summons without regard to the questions which have been raised in later times as to the precise nature of his authority. . . .

"It was in this way, by the holding of meetings at which both the ecclesiastical and civil elements were represented, and which dealt with ecclesiastical no less than with civil questions, that there grew up the conceptions of both ecclesiastical and political unity, which, more than physical force, welded together the divers populations of what are now Spain, France, and England, each into a single whole. The older Roman imperial arrangements lasted on, but only for limited purposes. The province was superseded by the nation in almost all respects, except that of internal discipline."[1] It is interesting to observe that the first consolidation of the English dioceses into a National

---

[1] Hatch, "The Growth of Christian Institutions," p. 152.

Church was a purely ecclesiastical act, without any royal assistance; the summoning of the Council of Hertford by the great Archbishop Theodore of Tarsus, which took place on September 24, 673.

The unity of primitive times was a unity of the main points of doctrine, not of uniformity of practice. Every Church was at liberty to make choice for herself in what method and form of words she would perform her services. It was no breach of unity for different Churches to have different modes and circumstances and ceremonies in performing the same holy offices so long as they kept to the substance of the institution. What was required to keep the unity of the Church in these matters was that any particular member of any Church should comply with the particular customs and usages of his own Church.[1]

The independence of National Churhes is illustrated by a primitive rule that every Christian, when he came to a foreign Church, should readily comply with the innocent usages and customs of that Church where he happened to be, though they might chance, in some circumstances, to differ from his own. "This was a necessary rule of peace, to preserve the unity of communion and worship throughout the whole Catholic Church; for it was impossible that every Church should have the same rites and ceremonies, the same customs and usages in all respects, or even the same method and manner of worship, exactly agreeing in all punc-

[1] Bingham, "Eccl. Antiq.," bk. xvi. § 10.

tilios with one another, unless there had been a general liturgy for the whole Church expressly enjoined by Divine appointment. The unity of the Catholic Church did not require this . . . and, therefore, no one ever insisted on this as any necessary part of its unity. It was enough that all Churches agreed in the substance of Divine worship; and for circumstantials, such as rites and ceremonies, method and order, and the like, every Church had liberty to judge and choose for herself by the rules of expediency and convenience." [1] The idea of one uniform Church throughout the world ✓ is merely an unconscious recollection of the long feverish dream of papal supremacy. "This rule is often inculcated by St. Austin as the great rule of peace and unity with regard to all Churches; and, he tells us, he received it as an oracle from the wise and moderate discourses of St. Ambrose, whom he consulted upon the occasion of a scruple which had possessed the heart of his mother, Monica, and for some time greatly perplexed her. She, having lived a long time at Rome, was used to fast on Saturday or the 'Sabbath,' according to the custom of the Church of Rome; but, when she came to Milan, she found the contrary custom prevailing, which was to keep Saturday a festival; and, being much disturbed about this, her son, though he had not much concern about such matters at that time, for her ease and satisfaction consulted St. Ambrose upon the point, to take his

[1] Bingham, "Eccl. Antiq.," bk xvi. § 10.

M

advice and direction how to govern herself in this case, so as to be inoffensive in her practice. To whom St. Ambrose answered, 'That he could give no better advice in the case than to do as he himself was wont to do; for,' said he, 'when I am here I do not fast on the Sabbath; when I am at Rome I fast on the Sabbath; and so you, whatever Church you come to, observe the custom of that Church, if you neither take offence at them nor give offence to them.' St. Austin says, 'This answer satisfied his mother, and he always looked upon it as an oracle sent from heaven.' He adds, moreover, 'That he had often experienced with grief and sorrow the disturbance of weak minds, occasioned either by the contentious obstinacy of certain brethren, or by their own superstitious fears, who, in matters of this nature, which can neither be certainly determined by the authority of Holy Scripture, nor by the tradition of the Universal Church, nor by any advantage in the correction of life, raise such litigious questions, as to think nothing right but what themselves do; only because they were used to do so in their own country; or because a little shallow reason tells them it ought to be so; or because they have, perhaps, seen some such thing in their travels, which they reckon the more learned the more remote it is from their own country.' Thus he wisely reflects upon the superstitious folly and contentious obstinacy of such as disturbed the Church's peace for such things as every Church had liberty to use, and every good Christian was obliged to comply with. 'For,' as he says in the same place, 'all such customs as varied in the practice of different Churches, as that some fasted on the Saturday, and others did not; some received the Eucharist every day, others on the Sabbath and the Lord's Day, and others on the Lord's Day only; and whatever else there was of this kind, they were all things of free observation; and in such things there could be no better rule for a grave and prudent Christian to walk by than to do as the Church did whenever he happened to come. For whatever was enjoined that was neither against faith nor good manners was to be held indifferent, and to be observed according to the custom and for the convenience of the society among whom we live.' This he repeats over and over again as the most safe rule of practice in all such things, wherein the customs of the Churches varied, that wherever we see any things appointed, or know them to be appointed, that are neither against faith nor good manners, and have any tendency to edification, and to stir men up to a good life, we should not only abstain from finding fault with them, but follow them both by our commendation and imitation. By this rule all wise and peaceable men always governed their practice in holding communion with other Churches; though they did not altogether like their customs, they did not break communion with them upon that account."[1]

[1] Bingham, "Eccl. Antiq.," bk. xvi. § 10.

In the same way, "A great many things were at first allowed to every bishop in the management of his own diocese, which were afterwards restrained by the decrees of national councils. As to instance only one in particular: every bishop anciently had liberty to frame his own liturgy for the use of his own Church.

"It is clear that there was no necessity, in order to maintain the unity of the Catholic Church, that all Churches should agree in all the same rites and ceremonies; but every Church might enjoy her own usages and customs, having liberty to prescribe for herself in all things of an indifferent nature, except where either a universal tradition or the decree of some general or national council intervened to make it otherwise. To this purpose is that famous saying of Irenæus, upon occasion of the different customs of several Churches in observing the Lent fast: 'We still retain peace one with another: and the different ways of keeping the fast only the more commends our agreement in the faith.' St. Jerome, likewise, speaking of the different customs of Churches in relation to the Saturday fast, and the reception of the Eucharist every day, lays down the general rule, 'That all ecclesiastical traditions, which did noways prejudice the faith, were to be observed in such manner as we had received them from our forefathers, and the custom of one Church was not to be subverted by the contrary custom of another; but every province might abound in their own sense, and esteem the rules of their ancestors as laws of the apostles.' After the same manner, St. Austin says, 'That in all such things, whereabout the Holy Scripture has given no positive determination, the custom of the people of God, or the rules of our forefathers, are to be taken for laws. For, if we dispute about such matters, and condemn the custom of one Church by the custom of another, that will be an eternal occasion of strife and contention; which will always be diligent enough to find out plausible reasonings, when there are no certain arguments to show the truth. Therefore great caution ought to be used, that we draw not a cloud over charity, and eclipse its brightness in the tempest of contention.' He adds a little after, 'Such contention is, commonly, endless, engendering strifes, and terminating in disputes. Let us therefore maintain one faith throughout the whole Church, wherever it is spread, as intrinsical to the members of the body, although the unity of the faith be kept with some different observations, which in noways hinder or impair the truth of it. For all the beauty of the King's daughter is within, and those observations which are differently celebrated, are understood only to be in her outward clothing; whence she is said to be clothed in golden fringes, wrought about with divers colours. But let that clothing be so distinguished by different observations as that she herself may not be destroyed by oppositions and contentions about them.' *This was the ancient way of preserving peace in the Catholic Church, to let different Churches, which had no dependence in externals upon one another, enjoy their own liberty to follow their own customs without contradiction.* As Gregory the Great said to Leander, a Spanish bishop, 'There is no harm done to the Catholic Church by different customs, so long as the unity of the faith is preserved;' and, therefore, though the Spanish Churches differed in some customs from the Roman Church, yet he did not pretend to oblige them to leave their own customs and usages, to follow the Roman. He gave a like answer to Austin the monk, Archbishop of Canterbury, when he asked him, 'What form of Divine service he should settle in Britain, the old Gallican or the Roman? And how it came to pass, that when there was but one faith, there were different customs in different Churches; the Roman Church having one form of service, and the Gallican Churches another?' To this he replied, 'Whatever you find either in the Roman or Gallican, or any other Church, which may be more pleasing to Almighty God, I think it best that you should carefully select it, and settle it in the use of the English Church, newly converted to the faith. For we are not to love things for the sake of the place, but places for the sake of the good things we find in them; therefore you may collect out of every Church whatever things are pious, religious, and right; and, putting them together, instil them into the minds of the English, and accustom them to the observation of them.' And there is no question but that Austin followed this direction in his new plantation of the English Church."[1]

"Neither was this liberty granted to different Churches in bare rituals, and things of an indifferent nature, but something in more weighty points, such as the receiving, or not receiving, those that were baptized by heretics and schismatics, without another baptism. This was a question long debated between the African, and Roman, and other Churches; yet without breach of communion, especially on their part who followed the moderate counsels of Cyprian, who still pleaded for the liberty and independency of different Churches in this matter, leaving all Churches to act according to their own judgment, and keeping peace and unity with those that differed from him.' This is further illustrated by the independency of Bishops, especially in the African Churches."[2]

Another instance of divergence and independence was the mode in which the Jewish Sabbath was treated. Some Churches, those of the Patriarchate of Antioch especially, not only observed the Christian Lord's Day, but also the Jewish Sabbath. On the other hand, some Churches used to fast on the Saturday, or Sabbath, as well as on the Friday, because on the former our Lord lay in the grave, as on the latter He was crucified.

[1] Bingham, "Eccl. Antiq.," bk. xvi. § 15.   [2] Ibid.

Some well-known points of divergence in the first three centuries were these:

1. The time of keeping Easter.
2. Was Saturday a fast or a feast?
3. Was Lent a period of forty hours, or forty days, or other different periods?
4. The variety of creeds.
5. The differences in the rules of provincial councils; *e.g.*, Elvira, Arles, and Ancyra.
6. Differences between churches in the East and West as to the canonicity of certain books of the New Testament.
7. The gradual adoption of the decrees of the general councils. They won their way progressively, by their intrinsic importance.
8. The number of ancient liturgies. Of these there are said to be no less than one hundred. Every bishop had at first power to draw up his own liturgy. They may be classified under five or six families, according to the Churches in which they were originally used; namely, those of Jerusalem (or Antioch), Alexandria, Constantinople, Ephesus, and Rome. They are also to be distinguished as those of the Oriental and the Occidental Churches.

It is, in fact, altogether impossible to use the word "Catholic" of any ecclesiastical custom. Catholic applies to truths and to institutions, but not to ceremonies. The definition of St. Vincent of Lérins, a well-known presbyter of Gaul, who died about 450

A.D., "quod semper, quod ubique, quod ab omnibus," will hold good of truths and institutions, but few if any ceremonies. It is difficult to claim for any mere ceremony so august a usage. Baptism and the Lord's Supper are institutions rather than ceremonies—something better than mere ceremonies themselves. They are themselves Catholic, but the way of celebrating them has greatly varied. The descriptions of Pliny, of Justin, of the "Teaching of the Twelve Apostles," and even of Cyril of Jerusalem, contain the germs of what has been elsewhere developed, but they are not identical with subsequent rites.

It is in accordance with these principles that the preface to our Book of Common Prayer lays it down "that the particular forms of Divine worship, and the rites and ceremonies appointed to be used therein, being things in their own nature indifferent, and alterable, and so acknowledged, it is but reasonable that, upon weighty and important considerations, according to the various exigency of times and occasions, such changes and alterations should be made therein, as to those that are in place of authority from time to time seem either necessary, or expedient."[1]

To the same effect is the Thirty-fourth Article on the traditions of the Church: "It is not necessary that traditions and ceremonies be in all places one, or utterly like; for at all times they have been divers, and may be changed according to the diversities of

[1] "The Preface to the Book of Common Prayer."

countries, times, and men's manners, so that nothing be ordained against God's Word. Whosoever through his private judgment, willingly and purposely, doth openly break the traditions and ceremonies of the Church, which be not repugnant to the Word of God, and be ordained and approved by common authority, ought to be rebuked openly (that others may fear to do the like), as he that offendeth against the common order of the Church, and hurteth the authority of the magistrate, and woundeth the consciences of the weak brethren.

"Every particular or national Church hath authority to ordain, change, and abolish ceremonies or rites of the Church ordained only by man's authority, so that all things be done to edifying."

In the same way our Book of Common Prayer, in the Preface on Ceremonies, declares that: "Although the keeping or omitting of a ceremony, in itself considered, is but a small thing; yet the wilful and contemptuous transgression and breaking of a common order and discipline is no small offence before God. 'Let all things be done among you,' saith St. Paul, 'in a seemly and due order.' The appointment of the which order pertaineth not to private men. Therefore no man ought to take in hand, nor presume to appoint or alter any public or common order in Christ's Church, except he be lawfully called and authorised thereto."

And again in the same introduction: "Christ's Gospel is not a Ceremonial Law (as much of *Moses*'

Law was), but it is a religion to serve God, not in bondage of the figure or shadow, but in the freedom of the Spirit: being content only with those ceremonies which do serve to a decent order and godly discipline, and such as be apt to stir up the dull mind of man to the remembrance of his duty to God, by some notable and special signification, whereby he might be edified."

And at the close of it: "And in these our doings we condemn no other nations, nor prescribe anything but to our own people only: For we think it convenient that every country should use such ceremonies as they shall think best to the setting forth of God's honour and glory, and to the reducing of the people to a most perfect and godly living, without error or superstition; and that they should put away other things, which from time to time they perceive to be most abused, as in men's ordinances it often chanceth diversely in divers countries."

When, therefore, men go behind the "Book of Common Prayer and Administration of the Sacraments and other Rites and Ceremonies of the Church according to the use of the Church of England," and speak of the customs or practices of a Catholic Church to which they owe allegiance, they are not only transgressing a principle of Catholic order, but they are talking of what absolutely does not exist, and is impossible. They mean only that there are certain rites and ceremonies which they admire long in vogue in the Roman Communion, or even going back to the time before the division between East and West, and now laid aside by the Church of England, which was forced, in the course of time, to declare its independence and autonomy.

Such, then, are the rights of National Churches: independence of jurisdiction, independence of custom, independence of ritual, independence of definition, so long as there is unity with the principles of the greatest and most important assemblies of the whole of the united Churches, such as the First Four General Councils, in subordination to the supreme authority of the word of God contained in Scripture. And as we are anxious that all Christians living in one nation should belong to the same pure and Apostolical Church, we should take good care, by only insisting strongly on things of primary importance, to make easy to them the way of return.

XI.

THE PRINCIPLES OF CHURCH MUSIC.

"Except ye utter by the tongue words easy to be understood, how shall it be known what is spoken? for ye shall speak into the air. There are, it may be, so many kinds of voices in the world, and none of them is without signification. Therefore if I know not the meaning of the voice, I shall be unto him that speaketh a barbarian, and he that speaketh shall be a barbarian unto me. Even so ye, forasmuch as ye are zealous of spiritual gifts, seek that ye may excel to the edifying of the church."—1 COR. xiv. 9-12.

THE element of simple joy and gladness was to be a leading part of the Christian life. He who had done with the world, and whose whole being was fixed on the anticipation of a glorious future, would spontaneously burst forth into happy songs of delight, as the lark cannot help carolling when it soars high and bathes itself in the rapturous glow of the sunshine. "Be ye filled with the Spirit," the Christians at Ephesus are told; "speaking to yourselves in psalms and hymns and spiritual songs, singing and making melody in your heart to the Lord."[1] "Let the word of Christ dwell in you richly in all wisdom,"

[1] Eph. v. 18.

it is said to the little flock at Colossæ; "teaching and admonishing one another in psalms and hymns and spiritual songs; singing with grace in your hearts to the Lord."[1] It was part of the common worship of that primitive time that every Christian who was so disposed, or who felt the gift within him, composed his own little sacred poem, or verse of praise, and brought it to the meeting, and chanted or recited it as the case might be. So great was the competition to sing these little original productions at Corinth, that St. Paul had gently to insist that there should be some order and method in the service.[2]

You will like to hear the beginning of the system which you see before you in choral services. Gradually the glowing energy of the Apostolic period died away, and the congregations settled down to more regular forms. By the time of the sixth century it seems to have been the custom for the presbyters and deacons themselves to execute the singers' part, the sub-deacons and inferior clerks chanting the Psalms; and this they often performed, as might be expected, very inefficiently. It was Gregory the Great,[3] the reformer of Church music, who seems to have established at Rome a regular choir school for the education

---

[1] Col. iii. 16. [2] 1 Cor. xiv. 26-40.
[3] "Life of Gregory the Great," by John the Deacon; Migne, *Patrol. Lat.* See *Conc. Rom.*, A.D. 395; *Decret. Greg.*, cap. i.; also "Dict. of Christian Antiq.," vol. ii. p. 1845, article *Schola Cantorum*.

of youths in ecclesiastical chant and sacred learning, who should be able, not to lead the praise at every religious assembly, but to sing the solemn offices at the several churches of the city on special and great occasions. It was governed by an officer of great dignity, who was sometimes called Prior of the Choir School, sometimes Precentor. The institution has been ascribed to previous Bishops of Rome; but at any rate it was Gregory the Great who endowed it, and constructed its own proper college or residence.[1] From Rome the new arrangement spread to other churches, so that by the time of Charlemagne we also find mention of such a choir school at Lyons.[2] In this school of Lyons, says their archbishop, several became so learned that they could even instruct others. It was King Pippin, the father of Charlemagne, who first took measures for the introduction of Roman chanters into France to instruct the Gallicans, who appear to have been far less skilled in the execution of this heavenly art. Among the several schools which thus came into being, that of Metz seems speedily to have acquired distinction. In the time of Charlemagne, it was said that, in proportion as the Roman chant surpassed that of Metz, so that of Metz surpassed

---

[1] Boy-singers are mentioned by the "Apostolic" Constitutions, by Basil and Chrysostom; the "Canonical singers," by the Council of Laodicea; and Eusebius describes a regular choir at Antioch in the time of Constantine. Jerome speaks of "adolescentuli quibus psallendi in ecclesiâ officium est."

[2] Ledrad., *Archiepisc. Lugd. in Ep. ad Car. Mag.*

that of the other schools of the Franks. Charlemagne himself ordered the establishment of such schools in suitable places throughout his empire, with the object of setting the bishops and presbyters free from the necessity of attending to the music, and so enabling them to execute their offices with the greater seemliness and dignity. A choir school of a somewhat similar character appears to have existed in Africa two hundred years before Gregory the Great. There is a touching story that, in the Arian persecutions, twelve of the children of such a school were tortured to make them renounce the orthodox faith, and were highly esteemed at Carthage for the strenuous resistance that they made.

My brothers, we have in these early beginnings the origin of the cathedral choirs and choristers' schools, which have brought sacred music to so great a perfection in subsequent ages and in our own times.

Now, in addressing myself to laymen, either as choirmen or congregation, on the present occasion, I would have you remember that, while there are certain principles in common to all choirs, which all choirs are bound to remember, unless they would fail in their very first duties, yet on the other hand there are certain broad distinctions between the choir of a cathedral and the choir of a parish church which it is equally fatal not to acknowledge.

Among the principles common to all choirs alike are *Reverence, Edification,* and *Distinctness.*

There can be no true *Reverence* unless all who take part in the service, whether the minister who intones or the men and boys who sing, habitually realise every moment that they are at the very footstool of the Almighty, and in His immediate presence. The absence of this consciousness that we are speaking to the Divine Being makes itself felt in a moment. No substitute can be offered for it, either by a pious and melodious drawl, or by sharp mechanical utterance. Words so given by the minister reach neither the ear of the Almighty nor the heart of the people. There is in them none of the penetrating thrill of real conscious reverence. The same difference can be felt when the choir realise to themselves the awful words which they are using, and when they do not.

For this end the prayer which is said with the singers in the vestry should be a real earnest supplication, not a mere shibboleth. I have heard it shouted, I have heard it gabbled; but not often have I heard it in those tones of reality which alone would be acceptable to the awful Being Who inhabiteth eternity. It is probably better said than intoned, because intoning in such circumstances is apt to become perfunctory. It is better varied in words as often as possible, because the stereotyped form of words becomes more like a charm than a prayer. Too often the stentorian and ear-splitting Amen shows how little impression it has made. Such an Amen should be exceedingly soft, like the simple humble words of a little child. The loud boisterous Amen is in truth a very insolent beginning for the humility and penitence of the worship of God.

Part of the reverence by which all the service should be characterised should be the whispered softness of the General Confession and of the Lord's Prayer, in whatever part of the service it comes. The note of the General Confession should be dropped, to show the difference of its associations; and it should never be greatly above a whisper. To hear merry-looking, chubby-faced choristers shouting with jubilant and reckless carelessness aloud to Almighty God that they are miserable sinners, and that there is no health in them, is indeed distressing, and a woeful, almost irreparable shock to the whole devotional spirit of the service. The Lord's Prayer, too, is so infinitely pathetic and solemn that it should always be said with extreme quietness; otherwise, as the words are so well known, the tendency will be, as, alas! is so often the case, to rattle them through like a meaningless jig. In the same way the distresses and sorrows of the human heart, which pour themselves out with such inexpressible tenderness in the Litany, should be rendered in a tone that is throughout gentle, devotional, and subdued.

When I speak of *Edification* in Church music, I mean what our Lord said about the day of rest, that it exists for man, and not man for it. The service, however beautiful, does not exist for itself, that it should be performed even with the greatest ideal perfection without regard to the worshippers. Prose and poetry, music and plain unmodulated speaking, are all alike to Him to Whose perfection and delight we can add nothing, and to Whom we can only offer ourselves. Some persons seem to have mistaken the Almighty as revealed in the Lord Jesus Christ for some sublime musical deity, like the Apollo of the Greeks, in whose honour the perfection of music must be perpetually offered, without reference to the woes and passions, the joys and griefs, the passing temporary incidents and emotions, of the frail human beings who are worshipping Him. That is not the view of St. Paul. All must be done to Edification, to the building up of God's people.[1] That is the sole point of view. A cathedral will edify in one way, a parish church in another. A cathedral, by the abundance of its resources, and by its daily and continuous practice, can offer a perfection of tone, a delicacy of harmony, a skilfulness of musical art, which will appeal to the highest faculties of educated men. A parish church will aim rather at encouraging all God's people to sing. But the beginning and end of the aim of both must be a thoroughly sympathetic, a thoroughly intelligent aim at Edification.

The third principle common to both sorts of choirs

[1] 1 Cor. xii. 7; xiv. 26; 2 Cor. xii. 19; Eph. iv. 12.

is *Distinctness*. No possible good can result from either cathedral or parish church unless the words are understood. This object is probably more easily attained in a cathedral, because of the greater perfection of the singers, and the greater space or medium through which the words are heard. But it should always be remembered that, just as by far the greater part of the population of the country are the working classes, so by far the greater part of our worshippers ought to be the working classes, and that they do not catch words or meanings so readily as those whose ear is fully practised and educated. Whether they are in our churches in great numbers or not makes no difference. They ought to be there. We ought to expect them to be there. All our preparations should be as if they were coming. They are by far the most important class of our fellow-Christians in the present day, even if it were only from the sheer weight of multitude. If we conduct our services as if we did not expect them, then they will not come. No trouble can be too great to spend on absolute distinctness of utterance, the avoidance of harsh and screaming resonance, the elimination of confusion and echo, the calculation of accuracy in effect. How strong and clear is St. Paul's rule on the subject! " Except ye utter by the tongue words easy to be understood, how shall it be known what is spoken? for ye shall speak into the air. There are, it may be, so many kinds of voices in the world, and none of them is without signification. Therefore if I know not the meaning of the voice, I shall be unto him that speaketh a barbarian, and he that speaketh shall be a barbarian unto me. Even so ye, forasmuch as ye are zealous of spiritual gifts, seek that ye may excel to the edifying of the church."[1]

The principles which are special to parish choirs are *simplicity, unselfishness,* and *modesty,* or the *absence of ambition.*

With regard to *Simplicity,* the greater part of the music should be such as in it even the humblest can join. The tunes of the hymns and chants should be well known and familiar, and all within the compass of average voices. They must not aim at the elaborateness of the cathedral choir, because their function is different. The function of the cathedral, except at the specially popular services, is to be a school of Church music in which the most cultivated can from time to time be moved, aroused, and delighted.[2] The function of the parish church is to persuade all to sing. The old fashion, which placed the organ at the west end of the church, was in this respect a help, because it gave support and encouragement to the congregation. An occasional anthem is an encourage-

---

[1] 1 Cor. xiv. 9–12.
[2] Even here there is the danger of approaching the dreamy sensuousness of opium, or Indian hemp, the mind being passive and inarticulate, while the half-animal psyche alone comes into play. This would not be the "understanding also" of St. Paul, nor the worship in "*pneuma*" of our Lord.

ment to the choir, and has a charm for even unlettered people, if the words have been previously read to them, and they know what it is about. But the parish choir has no time at its disposal for practice and perfection comparable to that which is available for the cathedral; and a bad anthem is a very bad thing indeed, so bad that it only excites pity, contempt, and ridicule, and a vehement desire for its absence. It is felt to be a blot on the service.

Connected with this principle of *simplicity* is softness. There are very few parish choirs that do not sing too loud. They do not reflect that the same body of voice which might sound heavenly and peaceful in St. Paul's Cathedral, would have an appalling and deafening effect in a smaller church. In the hymns, certainly, a good body of voice is needed, but in hardly any other part of the service is loudness on the part of the choir anything else but a distraction and a nuisance. The distinctness of which I spoke has nothing whatever to do with loudness. The tendency to loudness is almost a universal failing; it is no doubt a protection, though but a poor one, against flatness; but it would be well if the trouble spent on elaborateness were directed to the cultivation of precision of tone and a self-relying softness. It would be well if all choirs could study the exquisite effect of the hushed stillness and whispered solemnity of the beautiful choir of the Temple Church.

The next point is *unselfishness*. The temptation common to most choirs is to think more of their own wishes, skill, and progress than of the good of God's people. Unselfishness is a grace earnestly to be prayed for by choirmaster, organist, and singers. With the exception of the occasional anthem, which we have mentioned, and of special services on week-days for oratorios, when none need come who are not musical, it is of the very utmost importance that in all parish churches the majority of the music should be such as all the people can share and understand.[1] The main recommendation which Gregorian chants have is that, when once the people get hold of them, they sing them with heart and soul. The extraordinary effect should never be forgotten of the unison singing at the great Tabernacle of South London, and of the well-known church of St. James' Holloway in the north. There is the help of neither organ nor choir, but the people undertake all the music themselves, and sing like the sound of many waters, with all the magic sympathy of innumerable hearts united in earnestness. That need not be our ideal; but in no single Church ought the organist and choir either to ignore the congregation altogether,

[1] Compare St. Ambrose: "Well is the Church generally compared to the sea, which first . . . then, in the praying of the whole people together roars as it were with waves poured back; and then, in the antiphonal singing of the psalms, a united thunder as of waves bounds to and fro from the voices of men, women, maidens, and young children."

or to treat them as a nuisance. I would even go so far as to say that in every group of five or six churches there should be always one with a plain old-fashioned service for those who are not musical, and who now sometimes seek in vain for a place where they can worship God in their own way. And in all churches, if the congregation are to join in as we all so earnestly wish, the choir and organist must not object to their being slow.[1] The majestic style of the German chorale is far more encouraging to congregational music than the light, crisp, quick notes of much of our modern hymnody. You cannot expect people to join in sacred glees without much practice.

Lastly, there is the principle of *Modesty*, or the absence of ambition. The churches which can afford to have practised and skilful singers can adventure more than those that are in humbler circumstances, and are likely to be attended by congregations to whom more scientific music is intelligible and devotional. But the majority are not in this position, and it is much to be deplored if there should be a feeling that there can be but one fashion for all alike. If the clergy cannot intone well, it is infinitely preferable

---

[1] An acute friend of mine remarks: "Two sore evils under the sun are the practice of 'putting on the pace' to cut out the non-experts, to the utter obliteration of entire words and syllables; and the habit of changing tunes so that familiarity shall never be acquired, and the same words shall not go habitually to the same melodies."

that they should read rather than that they should intone badly. If the choir do not sing the responses, it is infinitely preferable that the responding should be left to the congregation, rather than that there should be a thin, poor, and rough monotoning on the part of those who have not the skill or experience to make their utterance musical and devotional. Ambition is the besetting sin of more than half our choirs; and a badly performed ambitious service, far from being an attractive influence, is a decided and absolute repulsion.

Deep is the gratitude we owe to our choirs for all the trouble and earnestness which they take on our behalf. Wonderful is the progress which music in our churches has made during the last half century, in consonance with the general advance in taste and education. True and real is the help which they give to our devotions. Inextinguishable is the obligation which we feel to the great masters of modern Church melodies, and to the poets whose hymns purify our thoughts, interpret our emotions, and rouse our best aspirations. Invaluable are our great musical festivals, when the choirs are trained by the most experienced minds, in the purest taste, and learn the majesty of concentrated praise. To carry on the work of the association, your generous sympathy and alms are asked. And may God, around whose glory the eternal melodies are ever echoing, grant to each of us, whether we are leaders or sharers in His Divine gift of music, whenever we meet before His invisible and omnipresent throne, to take in new draughts of spiritual life, because we have sought Him with a true service!

XII.

FASTING COMMUNION NOT OBLIGATORY.

"As they were eating, Jesus took bread, and blessed and brake it, and gave to the disciples, and said, Take, eat; this is My body."—ST. MATT. xxvi. 26 (R.V.).

THE minds of some earnest and devout members of our Church have, for some years past, been exercised by the question whether they ought not to follow what is declared by St. Augustine of Hippo, one of the greatest of the Fathers, the universal practice of the Church in his own day, that of fasting communion. Some have even wondered whether our mid-day Eucharist at St. Paul's, with its hundred communicants, was not slightly improper. And I have known candidates for Orders, imbued with these ideas, and not having broken their fast, actually faint at the end of a long ordination service. I desire, with the help of the Holy Spirit of God, to give them what assistance I can on this important subject.

St. Augustine died in the fifth century, in the year 430. His words are perfectly distinct: "It is beyond dispute," he wrote, "that when the disciples first received the body and blood of the Lord, they did not receive fasting. Are we, then, to blame the whole Church because every one does receive fasting? No; for it pleased the Holy Spirit that in honour of so mighty a sacrament the body of the Lord should pass the Christian's lips before other food, for it is on that account that that custom is observed throughout the whole world. . . . The Lord did not prescribe in what order it should be received, that He might reserve this privilege for the Apostles, through whom He was to regulate the Churches; for if He had recommended that it should be received after other food, I suppose none would have deviated from that practice." [1]

Now, in the first place, it is desirable to remember, as it has been put by a very learned Colonial prelate, Bishop Kingdon, Coadjutor of Fredericton, in a treatise which he wrote on this subject in the year 1873, that the authority of an individual Father, however great, is not absolute. He quotes the Roman Catholic historian, Fleury, to the effect that one of the causes of the relaxation of discipline and the corruption of manners in the later centuries, has been the taking for laws the opinions of individual doctors of the Church. "All must have observed that quotations from the Fathers are apt to be adduced as if they were conclusive on a subject, without respect being had to the particular value of the quotation. Such quotations must be received with respect, but they do not bind the conscience, nor do they necessarily cause censure to attach to those who do

[1] Augustine, Ep. 118, c. 6, p. 191, ed. Cologne, 1616.

not agree with them. . . . Such quotations show that certain opinions were held without blame, or that certain customs obtained, at the time of their being written. But in the matter of customs, that doctors of great name have spoken strongly in favour of them, does not necessitate their being continued always in the Church."

With regard to St. Augustine himself, deeply as we revere him, and highly as we value his immortal writings, we are not bound by all his opinions. His curious allegorising on the Old Testament, his exaggerated views on predestination and the absolute corruption of human nature, his rigorous asceticism, his forced and uncritical suggestion that St. Paul was the author of the obligation of fasting communion, his maintenance of the right of persecution—these were views incidental to his time, but which we are by no means compelled by our admiration of him to adopt.

Again, as to the age in which St. Augustine lived, it presents customs and doctrines which we no longer follow. It was an age when the celibacy of the clergy was strongly encouraged, though not actually, as yet, enjoined by authority. The superiority of monasticism was strenuously asserted. It was the age of Symeon the Stylite, who lived for thirty-six years on the top of a column; whose form of devotion, though followed by many others in that period, we do not now imitate. The practice of infant communion, then common, we have entirely dropped.

The exorcism of evil spirits in baptism was then universal. In certain churches no washing of the body was allowed during the forty days of Lent. It was an age with much to instruct us, but not one that demands implicit obedience to all its opinions and customs.

The fact is, that the most careful historians tell us that the necessity of communicating fasting does not appear to be distinctly recognised before the fourth century, the period in which St. Augustine was born.[1] However rapid, therefore, was the spread of the opinion of necessity, it cannot claim to fulfil two of the three requirements of catholicity. That alone is said to be catholic which has been held always, in all places, and by everybody. During the three most important centuries of the growth of the Christian Church the necessity of fasting communion does not appear.

If we look a little into the history of the hour of communion we shall see how the opinion of St. Augustine's days grew up to maturity. In the Apostolic age itself it is admitted by the Roman Catholic historian, Cardinal Baronius, that the communion took place at the time of supper, or the evening meal. And the Christians of those days had Apostolic example; for at Troas St. Paul broke bread after nightfall, and the service was not over

[1] "Dictionary of Christian Antiquities:" Holy Communion, vol. i. p. 418.

at midnight.¹ In the second century Justin Martyr shows, by his quotations from heathen calumnies, that the religious meetings of Christians took place in the same way after nightfall. As long as communion followed the *Agapè*, or common social meal, it is obvious that it was not received fasting.

But a gradual change took place in the tone of thought about the Holy Communion. The Offertory became more prominent than the Supper. The interpretation of our Lord's words became more carnal. The rite itself received new colouring and accessories. It gradually grew to be regarded as essential that both celebrant and recipients should be fasting at the time of their communion. Already, Tertullian, who died about 220, contrasts our Lord's practice with that in his own day.² But Cyprian, who was martyred in 258, by insisting on the greater worthiness of the morning communion, as compared with that in the evening, shows that the latter was not altogether obsolete.³

In the fourth century, we find Basil the Great, who was born in 329, urging what we may without offence describe as the non-apostolical view. "None," he says, "would venture to celebrate the mysteries otherwise than fasting."⁴ In the same way St. John Chrysostom,

---

¹ It is important to remember that this was owing to the extraordinary length of St. Paul's discourse. It was not an "early celebration," but an exceedingly late "Evening Communion."
² Tertullian, *De Coronâ*, cap. iii.
³ Cyprian, *Ep.* 63, cc. 15 and 16.
⁴ Basil, Hom. ii., *De jejunio*, p. 13.

who was born in 347, a few years before St. Augustine, declares that fasting is a necessary preliminary to worthy communion.[1] Those who are not fasting, he urges to come to church, not indeed to communicate, but to hear the sermon. Certain calumniators, he says, had charged him with receiving to communion those who were not fasting; this he denies, with the strongest asseverations. But he displays the grandeur of his mind, rising above these mere human restrictions, when he continues: "If they still go on to repeat their objection, let them degrade St. Paul, who baptized a whole house after supper; let them also depose the Lord Himself, who, after supper, gave the communion to His disciples."

St. Chrysostom, in spite of the language which he used to accommodate the prevailing prejudice of his day, clearly regarded the matter as a rule of men, not as a Divine ordinance. And it should be remembered that when St. Augustine said that the whole Church received fasting, he was using rhetorical language. A correspondent had asked him what he was to do on Thursday in Holy Week, when the Church always celebrated an evening communion, after a feast, in commemoration of the original institution.[2] Was he to communicate on that day in the morning or in the evening, or at both? St. Augustine is obliged

[1] Chrysost. in 1 Cor., *Hom.* 27, p. 231.
[2] *Codex Canonum Eccl. Afric*, Canon 41; III. *Concil. Carthage*, c. 29.

to admit in his answer that the Church did not condemn communion on Holy Thursday after the evening meal. But if he made that admission, how could fasting communion be a matter of principle? And more than that. The historian of the early Church, who bears the same name as the sage of Athens, Socrates, mentions that the churches of the province that bordered on Alexandria and the Thebaid communicated, like other churches, on Saturday, but contrary to the general custom, preserved the Apostolical habit of taking previously their evening meal without stint.[1] The custom, however widely spread, was clearly not actually universal.

St. Augustine, notwithstanding his strong language about fasting, most distinctly taught that our Lord's words as to eating His body are a figure. And it was not till the ninth century that a Frankish monk, Paschasius, caused a vehement controversy in the Frankish Church, by teaching for the first time the doctrine of the Real Corporal Presence.[2] But in the sixth century regulations began to be made by synodical councils in Gaul enforcing fasting communion. Now, here it is highly important to remember that there are different kinds of Church councils. There are general councils, national councils, provincial councils, and councils diocesan. Even general councils may err,

[1] Socrates, "Hist. Eccl.," v. 22, p. 295.
[2] Robertson, "Hist. of the Christian Church," vol. ii. (ed. 1868), pp. 250, 259, 304-5, 392, 655.

as our own Church insists in her Articles; but their decisions are entitled to receive, at any rate, the greatest respect. But even in general councils, the canons of discipline are always held to differ from the canons of faith. The canons of discipline may vary with time and place; they are not everywhere binding. St. Augustine himself points out that the canon of the Apostles against eating things strangled was passed out of deference to the Jewish Christians, and had long ceased to be in force. But when we come to these canons of the Church of Gaul and other local Churches, passed at Carthage in Africa, Braga in Spain, Macon and Auxerre in France, Toledo in Spain, and one in the Emperor's palace at Constantinople, these have no force at all beyond their own diocese or province.[1] An English canon of 960 enjoins fasting communion on the laity. In 1549 the Council of Mayence insists that communion must not be given to non-fasters.

There was, indeed, a rule in the Book for Penitents put forth by Archbishop Theodore in the seventh century in England, that those who communicated otherwise than fasting were to fast seven days afterwards; but that, probably, only throws light on the meaning of the word "fasting" at that period.[2] These persons could not abstain from all food for a whole

---

[1] For these Councils, see "Dict. of Christian Antiquities," Holy Communion, p. 418, and Landon's "Manual of Councils."
[2] Bishop Kingdon on "Fasting Communion."

week; they were ordered to abstain from all but light food. And even that restriction was not in every case binding; for that shrewd archbishop, knowing the habits of our Anglo-Saxon forefathers, allowed them, instead of fasting, to repeat psalms. And these rules of Archbishop Theodore do not appear to have been subsequently enforced. Even if a canon of some Saxon king or council were discovered, it has been obsolete for ages. The canons of the foreign provincial Churches about fasting communion were never introduced into England. And even if they had been, it is a well-known principle of canon law that canons which are not directly enforced become nugatory by disuse, even after the short period of forty years.[1]

The wonderful variety which was recognised and encouraged in different churches in the earlier and more exemplary ages of Christendom, is a fact which some of us are apt in these days to forget. "History tells us that the Catholic Church is made up of particular local Churches, whose customs have varied without breach of unity. History and the canons of the Church show that particular Churches may have their own liturgies, and introduce alterations in them; may have customs different at different times, without there being any necessary danger to inter-communion." In primitive times the Churches did not keep Easter at the same date. Some kept Saturday as a feast, others as a fast. Some considered Lent a period of

[1] Bishop Kingdon on "Fasting Communion."

forty hours, others of forty days. At one time almost every Church had a different creed. The East and the West did not agree for three centuries as to the authority of certain of the books of the New Testament. Every bishop had the power of drawing up his own prayer-book; at least, a hundred different liturgies can be traced. "History tells us that canons of discipline, and customs unsanctioned by canons, or not enforced by them, have been constantly allowed to fall into disuse by particular Churches without endangering unity. If, therefore, we believe the Church of England to be indeed a living part of the True Vine, we need not fear to accept her relaxation of an ancient custom, when the reason of that custom has been removed by entire change of manners."[1]

The reason of that custom amongst the ancients was that they had fewer meals in the day, and at these they were accustomed to eat far more than is now our custom. St. Clement of Alexandria describes persons "more like swine or dogs for gluttony than men, in such a hurry to feed themselves full that both jaws are stuffed out at once, the veins about the forehead raised, and besides, the perspiration running all over, as they are tightened with their insatiable greed, and panting with their excess." St. Chrysostom, in one of his Lenten sermons, warns his hearers "to be careful, though perchance with reluctance, of the duty of sobriety

[1] Bishop Kingdon on "Fasting Communion."

before coming to church; and not to be led away at any time into excess of wine and gluttony. For the thought and expectation of entering the church should teach them to make such use of food and drink as accords with decency: lest after they had come there they should appear ridiculous to all present by smelling of wine, and unmannerly eructation." Elsewhere the same saint praises a Christian lady for not over-eating herself. "It must, then, be remembered that in times when fasting communion was the custom, excess in eating was the rule, and not the exception; and in order that men might come reverently to communion, it was natural that the rule should be that they should come fasting."[1] And the rule applied not only to communion, but to baptism, confirmation, and ordination, for the same reason of excessive eating, whether as bishop, priest, catechumen, or candidate. So different were those times from ours.[2]

Four more differences must be remembered. The first is that the ancients did not always mean the same thing by fasting that we mean by complete abstinence. St. Basil's description of fasting is based on the temperate habits of the Nazarite and the

[1] The introduction of coffee and tea has made a great difference in this respect. In the Middle Ages beer was the common beverage at breakfast. Subsequent temporary obfuscation amongst illiterate people (the vast majority) would be not unusual. Barbaric rules have lost their fitness.
[2] Ibid.

Levitical priesthood. This would exclude eating to excess, but not the ordinary modern early repast. St. Augustine himself says that the most severe fasters of his day used to eat in the night. A man who should communicate at a mid-day service, after a light early meal, would be held to be, in the more general sense of the word, "fasting." We ourselves use the word of those who take light instead of heavy food during Lent. The second additional difference is that the periods of their day and their night varied by some hours from our own. The discovery of new mineral oils, gas, and electric light has worked a wonderful change in the course of this century. In St. Augustine's days they had nothing but small oil lamps. They retired to rest soon after darkness set in, and the hours of work began at four or five o'clock in the morning. Nine o'clock was like twelve of noon with ourselves.

The third difference is, that there is no evidence to show that in the days of St. Augustine it would be held that a strict fast should begin at twelve o'clock in the night. That is a more recent refinement, the origin of which we do not know. Even in mediæval days, a man was held to be fasting, in the strictest sense, who had not eaten for three hours, when digestion might be considered to be complete. St. Augustine indeed says that the bread and wine of the Eucharist were to be the first food to pass the lips; but since what point of time we are left to conjecture.

The fourth additional difference is that of climate. The climate of North Africa and of the Mediterranean churches known to St. Augustine, was warm, bright, and sunny; severity of fasting in such a climate was easy and natural. Colder climates require more constant food. More instances of prolonged fasting are to be found in the East. The excessive work, says Bishop Kingdon, crowded into the day, at all events, in London and the other large towns of England, renders more frequent food necessary; and it is to be gravely doubted whether a minister, who lies in bed till eleven o'clock if he has to celebrate at mid-day, in order that he may have fasted from midnight with impunity, is serving God with his time as well as one who takes a light breakfast to enable him to do some work for God before mid-day. And it must be remembered that, if a man wished to satisfy all the mediæval canons of foreign churches, he would have to fast for six hours after receiving communion, as well as the previous abstinence.

There is one view of this supposed obligation which was repudiated with earnest and indignant warmth by the illustrious Bishop Samuel Wilberforce. I should have thought it almost needless to oppose such an opinion, because, as we saw, the doctrine of the Real Corporal Presence was not introduced till the ninth century, when it was taught in France by Paschasius. It can have nothing to do with our

Reformed Church, which in catechism, and article, and communion office insists with reiterated force on the spiritual character of the Divine Presence. But we know that there was reason for what was said by that great prelate. He pointed out that the practice was not advocated because a man came in a clearer spirit, and with less disturbed body and mind, able to give himself entirely to prayer and communion with his God, but on a miserable, degraded notion that the consecrated elements would meet with other food in the stomach. It was, he declared, a detestable materialism. Physically, it was a contradiction, because, when the celebration was over, the man might hurry away to a meal, and the process about which he was so scrupulous immediately followed. The whole notion, he added, was simply disgusting.

The result of these human restrictions was that up to the time of the Reformation very few men ever communicated. Even St. Chrysostom complained that they stood close enough in church to hear him preach, but almost all left the church without communicating. To suit this unhappy state of things the canons began to insist on only three communions in the year; Christmas, Easter, Pentecost. Then it came down to once a year, Easter; then it was alleged conveniently that these were only church regulations, and that by Divine ordinance one reception in a lifetime was enough: that on the deathbed.

Our beloved Church at the Reformation set about

to remedy this sad declension from primitive times; and she remedied it by distinctly not insisting on fasting communion. Faith, repentance, charity, good resolutions she requires, not preparatory abstinence. "That the Lord's Supper," said Bishop Jeremy Taylor, "is sacredly and with reverence to be received is taught us by the Apostles; but whether this reverence ought to be expressed by taking it fasting or not fasting, the Apostles left the Churches to their choice."[1]

If it is urged that such a difference from the canons of the Church of Rome is a hindrance to any possible reunion of Christendom in the future, the answer is, that so is the marriage of ministers, so is giving the cup to the laity, so is every one of the just and righteous corrections which at the Reformation we were compelled to make of mediæval errors.

Well may the Bishop of Fredericton ask, "By what right could an individual priest say that to communicate after any food is 'that which God has forbidden,' 'a service which there is great reason to fear He will never accept?'" To such an one St. Chrysostom would address his scathing words, 'Let them degrade the Lord Himself, who after supper gave the communion to His Apostles.' Let them excommunicate the Apostles for receiving after their meal. By what right do the priests in England say, as some constantly do, that to communicate otherwise

[1] *Virgine salivâ.*

than fasting is a mortal sin? By no right, human or Divine. If they know the meaning of what they say, surely they are making the heart of the righteous sad whom God hath not made sad ; if they do not know the meaning, it is unpardonable in them to use such language."

It is the duty of us all to come to the Holy Communion in as devout and earnest a frame of mind as God's Holy Spirit will permit. To some an early communion without food will be a help; to others, even this would be a hindrance. There is no rule on the subject. The English Church knows no canon in the matter. The canons of foreign churches bind only themselves. No general council recognised by us has spoken on the case at all. Holy Scripture is altogether silent; its evidence points the other way. The Church of England lays down in her Sixth Article that whatsoever is not read in Holy Scripture nor may be proved thereby, is not to be thought requisite or necessary to salvation; in her Twentieth Article she affirms that the Church ought not, beside Scripture, to enforce anything to be believed for necessity of salvation; and she exacts from all priests at their ordination a promise that they will teach nothing as required of necessity to eternal salvation, but that which they shall be persuaded may be concluded and proved by the Scripture. Then, my brothers, stand firm in the liberty wherewith Christ has made you free. If any think abstinence is better for themselves, let them fast; but let them not force their opinion upon others. For ages may our holy mid-day feast of thanksgiving at St. Paul's be the message of the Lord Jesus Christ to many a humble and faithful recipient! May the numbers of rejoicing communicants continually increase till there are not clergy enough to administer to them the pledges of God's love! May we at length return to the zeal and loyalty of primitive days, when none denied themselves that high privilege, or went empty away!

Note.—Appended are the Resolutions of the Bishops of the Province of Canterbury, at their sitting on May 5, 1893 :—

1. That in the Apostolic age the Holy Communion was administered in connection with the gathering together of Christians to share in an appointed evening meal.

2. That the practice of communicating in the early morning appears to have arisen about the close of the first century, probably in order to secure a safer as well as a more reverent celebration, and, by the time of St. Cyprian, to have become so fully established that it was regarded not only as the preferable, but as the proper practice, and as commemorative of the Lord's Resurrection.

3. That the practice of communicating in the early morning, together with the common association of fasting with prayer, led to the practice of communicating only when fasting, and that fasting reception of the Communion became the regular and recognised usage of the Church before the end of the fourth century.

4. That from the close of the fourth century this regular and recognised usage was formulated in rules for the clergy in canons of local and provincial councils.

5. That fasting reception of the Communion was the prescribed rule of the Church of England during the Anglo-Saxon period, and continued to be so to the time of the Reformation.

6. That these strict rules were, nevertheless, subject to relaxation in cases of sickness or other necessity.

7. That at the Reformation the Church of England, in accordance with the principle of liberty laid down in Article XXXIV., ceased to require the Communion to be received fasting, though the practice was observed by many as a reverent and ancient custom, and as such is commended by several of her eminent writers and divines down to the present time.

8. That, regard being had to the practice of the Apostolic Church in this matter, to teach that it is a sin to communicate otherwise than fasting, is contrary to the teaching and spirit of the Church of England.

XIII.

THE SCRIPTURAL VIEW OF HOLY COMMUNION.

"We must take heed, lest, of the memory, it be made a sacrifice; lest, of a communion, it be made a private eating; lest, of two parts, we have but one; lest, applying it to the dead, we lose the fruit that be alive."—"Homily on Worthy Receiving."

"That it should be given to man instrumentally by hand and tongue to create God; to turn common bread and common wine, by a few movements of the hand, and a few utterances of the lips, into the very body and blood of Him who made the worlds; this was the keystone of that arch of priestly domination which once bestrode the world."—DEAN VAUGHAN, "Liturgy and Worship of the Church of England," p. 224.

IT is important that we should remember that there are many means of grace. There is the rite of washing, which our Lord Himself ordained as by the outward form of admission to His Church on the condition of faith and repentance. There is our own conscious turning towards God, when we receive His sanction and seal to our profession of service. There is our own private intercourse with our Father in heaven and our compassionate Saviour. There is the common worship of Christian men and women in the sanctuary of God. There is listening to the preaching of His Word. There is the private study of His written revelation. There is quiet meditation on the mysteries of existence. There is the attitude of patient expectant receptivity towards His Divine Spirit. There is the contemplation of the encouragements to our faith given in the lives of His saints. There is the help which we get through the advice given us by experienced men of God. There is the spirit of reasonable enthusiasm, which arises from united praise. There is the sympathy which all His servants feel for ideas and facts that are true and noble. There is that doing the will of God, of which our Lord spoke, in earnest and diligent philanthropy, by which, as He told us, we should know of the doctrine. There is the making to ourselves friends of the Mammon of Unrighteousness. God's grace means His help and inspiration, and it can come to us in these and many other ways.

Now, there is one simple ordinance which our Lord Jesus Christ left us, which seems to sum up in itself many of these means of grace. It was instituted on the solemn occasion of the last farewell supper, and was intended to ensure the remembrance of the Lord's one historical atoning sacrifice, and to enable us more distinctly and completely to share in the blessings secured to us by that Divine act of redemption. The primitive Christians obeyed our Lord's directions with entire and loyal simplicity. "This cup is the New Testament in My blood; this do, as oft as ye shall drink it in remembrance of Me."[1] At first

[1] 1 Cor. xi. 25.

it appears, in every family the one principal meal of the day was thus consecrated to the memory of the Redeemer and to communion with His Divine Presence.[1] And it is one of the few forms of Christian common worship which St. Paul describes.

There is another form, about which he is no less anxious, which appears to be founded on the worship of the synagogue, the meeting for reading, for prayer, for praise, for the delivery of exhortations, and for the exercise of the gift of tongues.[2] It is on this custom of worship that has grown up our practice of morning and evening prayer with the preaching of the Word.

The Primitive Church did not retain its early love and purity in such a degree as to enable them to preserve the habit of the consecrated meal. The disorders attendant upon it are noticed by St. Paul, and the holy commemoration gradually became more of a service. Forms of arranging the service became usual, and are numerous in the following ages. These became more and more ceremonious and obscure, until at the time of the Reformation our present service was reconstructed on the more ancient models and in harmony with Scripture itself.

It is one of the greatest misfortunes in the history of Christendom that this, the simplest and most touching of all ordinances, uniting us to the very days of our Lord Himself, should, through the ambiguities of

---

[1] Acts ii. 42, 46; xx. 7; 1 Cor. xi. 20; Tertullian, *De Oratione*.
[2] 1 Cor. xiv. 23.

human language and the tendencies of human corruptions, have become the battleground of party warfare. It is not difficult to understand what our Lord meant by it Himself.

First, in His earlier teaching, union of His peoples with Himself in heart and soul and spirit was constantly before His mind.[1] When He had been speaking of Himself in His accustomed figurative manner as the Bread of Life, and had explained that this Bread was His flesh, which He would give for the life of this world, the Jews, who wished to understand Him, were perplexed. How can this Man give us His flesh to eat? And He, determining that this deep truth should sink into their hearts, drove the seeming paradox further home: "Verily, verily, I say unto you, except ye eat the flesh of the Son of Man, and drink His blood, ye have no life in you. Whoso eateth My flesh and drinketh My blood hath eternal life; and I will raise him up at the last day. For My flesh is meat indeed, and My blood is drink indeed. He that eateth My flesh and drinketh My blood dwelleth in Me and I in him. As the living Father hath sent Me, and I live by the Father, so he that eateth Me, even he shall live by Me."[2] It was a hard saying for the Jews; they murmured; from that time many of His disciples went back and walked no more with Him. They misunderstood Him altogether. But since the Cross of Calvary we have had

---

[1] John vi. 35, &c.   [2] John vi. 53, &c.

less difficulty. Christ was the true Lamb of God taking away the sin of the world.[1] Christ our Passover was sacrificed for us.[2] As the Hebrews showed their faith in God's mercy by all partaking of the Paschal Lamb, so must we.[3] And this the Jews could not do when He spoke to them, because there He was before them.[4] This the disciples could not do in the Upper Chamber, because there He was talking to them and not yet crucified. But in His pitiful love He gave us emblems of His body and blood, by partaking of which we might concentrate our thoughts on His sacrifice, and become receptive of His special presence and grace. It was not actual flesh and blood that He meant, either bodily or spiritual; it is the Spirit that quickeneth, was His commentary on His own words, the flesh profiteth nothing; the words that I speak unto you, they are spirit and they are life. To the end that we should always remember the exceeding great love of our Master and only Saviour Jesus Christ thus dying for us, and the innumerable benefits which, by His precious bloodshedding, He hath obtained for us—He hath instituted holy mysteries as pledges of His love, and for a continual remembrance of His death, to our great and endless comfort.[5] Then is our faith strongest, then is our recollection sincerest, then are our thoughts most concentrated, then is our humility truest, then is our

[1] John i. 29. [2] 1 Cor. v. 7. [3] Exod. xii. 3–8.
[4] John vi. 63. [5] Address in the Communion Service.

repentance deepest, then is our need clearest, then is our opportunity most available, then is His grace most directly covenanted, then is His presence most felt within us, then is His promise most justly claimed.

It is sometimes said that our Lord is perpetually engaged in offering up His sacrifice in heaven. This is mistaken language, and contradicts the article of the Creed, which teaches that our Lord is set down on the right hand of God.[1] There is no separate heavenly act of intercession described in the New Testament; it is His loving presence wherever He is, with all the force of what He did on earth, that is the intervening power. There is no need for Him now to make a daily sacrifice, says the Epistle to the Hebrews: "Every priest standeth daily ministering and offering ofttimes the same sacrifices, which can never take away sins; but this man, after He had offered one sacrifice for sin for ever, sat down on the right hand of God."[2] Can any language be conceived more abundantly clear? "He needeth not daily, as those high priests, to offer up sacrifice first for His own sins and then for the people's: for this He did once, when He offered up Himself."[3] Can anything be more explicitly and peremptorily exclusive of the idea of the perpetually offered sacrifice? "He made there, by His one oblation of Himself once offered, a

---

[1] Article IV., Heb. i. 3; viii. 1; x. 12; xii. 2; Eph. i. 20; 1 Pet. iii. 22.
[2] Heb. x. 11-14.   [3] Heb. vii. 7.

full, perfect, and sufficient sacrifice, oblation, and satisfaction for the sins of the whole world."[1]

It is here that our Roman friends, and those who think with them, have departed from the Epistle to the Hebrews. The English Church, whose Orders we bear, reminds us that "the offering of Christ once made is that perfect redemption, propitiation, and satisfaction for the sins of the whole world, both original and actual; and there is none other satisfaction for sin, but that alone. Wherefore the sacrifice of Masses, in which it was commonly said that the priest did offer Christ for the quick and dead, to have remission of pain or guilt, were blasphemous fables and dangerous deceits."[2] The sacrifice was complete, once for all; it is the effect of it that is eternal, and wherever our Lord is, there is the force and meaning of the effect. "Our great High Priest, unlike Aaron, when He enters the Holiest of Holies in the true sanctuary, mounts the throne. The true Aaron merges into the true Melchizedek. When the Throne of Grace is approached, upon it or beside it the Royal Priest is found seated, like the Shekinah above the Ark, to dispense the blessings of His sacrifice once offered and for ever perfect. The great Epistle to the Hebrews insists on the fact that not only the sacrifice, but the offering of it, is over for ever; while the royal, high-priestly intercession and benediction based upon it are present and continuous. In His character as Priest it is necessary that this man should have

[1] Prayer of Consecration.   [2] Article XXXI.

somewhat to offer; and what that is, is explained to us in a later verse: 'He through the eternal Spirit offered Himself without spot to God.' The Holiest of Holies on earth had no altar; by passing into the holiest place in heaven our Lord shows that His sacrifice was without the camp—' Christ is not entered into the Holy places made with hands, which are the figures of the true, but into heaven itself, now to appear in the presence of God for us; nor yet that He should offer Himself often, as the High Priest entereth into the Holy Place every year, with blood of others; for then must He often have suffered since the foundation of the world. But now in the end of the world hath He appeared to put away sin by the sacrifice of Himself. And as it is appointed unto men once to die, but after this the judgment; so Christ was once offered to bear the sins of many.'"[1] Wherever He is, His Presence is a lasting appeal to that unique and solitary act.

We have in these days to defend the freedom of English Christianity, to maintain the doctrine of the one oblation of Christ finished upon the Cross, never to be continued or repeated. The teaching which is very generally given by the adherents of the mediæval movement that is amongst us is contained in the second chapter of the 22nd session of the Council of Trent. It is in the following words: "Since the same Christ who once offered Himself by His blood on the cross is contained in this Divine sacrifice, which is celebrated in

[1] Moule, "Outlines of Christian Doctrine."

the Mass, and offered without blood, the Holy Scripture teaches us that this sacrifice is really propitiatory, and made by Christ. . . . For assuredly God is appeased by this oblation . . . for the sacrifice which is now offered by the ministry of the priests is one and the same as that which Christ then offered on the cross, only the mode of offering is different. And the fruits of that bloody oblation are plentifully enjoyed by means of this unbloody one."

The language in the Canon of the Council of Trent in nowise differs from the language of our mediæval friends, when in their twelve hundred churches they return thanks to Almighty God for being permitted to offer unto Him Christ's perpetually pleaded sacrifice. The fact is, that as praise, almsgiving, and self-devotion are called sacrifice in the New Testament, the word "sacrifice" and the word "altar" became used in very early times in connection with the Lord's Supper, and these words having been once introduced, and having come into ordinary usage, suffer the usual fate of ambiguities. With the progress of doctrinal corruption, there came in the idea of expiatory sacrifice offered by the priests on the altar; and as with the doctrine of Transubstantiation, so with this. After centuries of oscillating and contradictory language, the doctrine of the propitiatory sacrifice of the Eucharist became generally established. But as we have seen, there is no sacrifice at all in Holy Communion in the propitiatory sense of the word. One of the greatest of English theologians, Archdeacon Waterland, in a very important chapter, enumerates eight sacrifices strictly according to the language of the Gospel: [1]—

1. The sacrifice of alms to the poor.
2. The sacrifice of prayer.
3. The sacrifice of praise.
4. The sacrifice of a true heart.
5. The sacrifice of ourselves.
6. The sacrifice by the Church of itself to Christ.
7. The offering up of true converts by their minister.
8. The sacrifice of faith, life, and self-humiliation in commemorating the death of Christ.

These are the sacrifices which we offer at all times to God. In Holy Communion we offer the sacrifice of praise and thanksgiving, and we offer ourselves in accordance with the language of St. Paul.

With regard to the nature of the presence of our Lord at His Holy Supper, the teaching of our Church is no less plain. It is by faith in the hearts of the receivers, not in the bread and wine itself, which are hallowed emblems of the one great sacrifice. Nobody is more responsible for our present Prayer-book than Archbishop Cranmer; and this is what he said about it in his most serious moments in controversy with the Romanists, "Christ is but spiritually present in the ministration of the Sacrament, and you say that He is,

---

[1] Waterland, "Doctrine of the Eucharist" (Ed. 1880), pp. 481, 482.

after a spiritual manner, in the Sacrament."[1] "Christ is not in the bread, neither spiritually, as He is in man, nor corporally as He is in heaven, but only sacramentally—as a thing may be said to be in the figure by which it is signified." "The effect of godly eating is the communication of Christ's Body and Blood, but to the faithful receiver, and not to the dumb creatures of bread and wine, under whose forms the Catholic faith teacheth not the Body and Blood of Christ invisibly to be hidden." In the same way Ridley taught: "The Body of Christ is communicated and given, not to the bread and wine, but to them which worthily do receive the Sacrament."[2] "Not that Christ hath transfused grace into the bread and wine." And Bishop Jewell,[3] "We are plainly taught by the Catholic learned Fathers to put a difference between the Sacrament and the Body of Christ; and that one of them is not really lapped up or shut within the other." "Christ is present with us of His part 'only by His grace'; of our part 'only by our faith'; by the Sacraments, only as by means of outward instruments, to move our sense." Bishop Jeremy Taylor, "By spiritually, they (the Romanists) mean present after the manner of a spirit, by spiritually we mean 'present to our spirits only'; that is, so as Christ is not present to any other presence but that of faith, or

---

[1] Cranmer's Works (Parker Society), i. 155; "Answer to Gardiner," pp. 91, 36, 238, 100.
[2] Works (Parker Society), pp. 240, 241.
[3] Ibid. ii. 602; i. 122; iii. 488.

spiritual susception; but their way makes His body to be present no way but that which is impossible, and implies a contradiction—a body not after the manner of a body, a body like a spirit, a body without a body,[1] and a sacrifice of a body and blood without blood."

Let me quote to you also the greatest of all English divines, Richard Hooker :[2] "The real presence of Christ's blessed Body and Blood is not to be sought for in the Sacrament, but in the worthy receiver of the Sacrament; and with this the very order of our Saviour's words agreeth ; first, 'Take and eat,' then 'This is My Body which is broken for you'; first, 'Drink ye all of this'; then followeth, 'This is My Blood of the New Testament, which is shed for many for the remission of sins.' I see not which way it should be gathered by the words of Christ, when and where the Bread is His Body, or the cup His Blood, but only in the very heart and soul of him that receiveth them. . . . It appeareth not that of all the ancient Fathers of the Church any one did ever conceive or imagine other than only a mystical participation of Christ's both Body and Blood in the Sacrament, neither are their speeches concerning the change of the elements themselves into the Body and Blood of Christ, such that a man can thereby in conscience assure himself that it was their meaning to persuade the world either of a corporal consubstantiation of Christ with those sanctified and blessed elements

---

[1] Real Presence, secs. 1-8.
[2] Hooker, *Eccl. Pol.* V., lxvii. 6, 12.

before we receive them, or of the like transubstantiation of them into the Body and Blood of Christ."

So St. Augustine: "This is to eat that meat and to drink that drink; even for a man to dwell in Christ and to have Christ dwelling in him; and, therefore, whoso dwelleth not in Christ, and in whom Christ dwelleth not, without doubt neither doth eat His flesh, nor drink His blood."[1]

Listen also to Bishop Beveridge:[2] "Scripture and Fathers holding forth so clearly that whosoever worthily receives the Sacrament of the Lord's Supper doth certainly partake of the Body and Blood of Christ, the devil thence took occasion to draw men into an opinion that the Bread which is used in that Sacrament is the very Body that was crucified upon the Cross, and the wine after consecration the very Blood which gushed out of His pierced side. The time when this opinion was first broached was in the days of Gregory III., Bishop of Rome."

Once more let me quote Waterland.[3] "The words 'Verily and indeed taken and received by the faithful' are rightly interpreted of a real participation of the benefits purchased by Christ's death. The Body and Blood of Christ are taken and received by the faithful, not corporally, not internally, but 'verily and indeed'—that is, effectually. The sacred symbols are no bare signs, no untrue figures of a thing absent; but the force, the

---

[1] *Super Joann.*, Tract 26.   [2] Beveridge, on Article XXVIII.
[3] Waterland, " Doctrine of the Eucharist," chaps. vi. and vii.

grace, the virtue, and benefits of Christ's body broken and blood shed—that is, of His Passion—are really and effectually present with all them that receive worthily. This is all the real presence that our Church teaches."

Lastly, let me place before you the words of one of the most learned of our modern bishops, one of the most rigid and austere of our theologians, Christopher Wordsworth, Bishop of Lincoln. In commenting on the Epistle to the Hebrews, he says: "If the Apostle had supposed that Christ's body and blood is offered as a sacrifice on the Christian altar on earth, he would not surely have omitted to say so in describing the Christian altar and the Christian sacrifice."[1]

Such is the position of Holy Communion in Christian worship. It is a chief and important means of grace, co-ordinate with others, foremost among many, a commemoration of the atoning sacrifice of the death of Christ, and a means of appropriating the benefits which we obtain thereby.

[1] Wordsworth's Commentary, *Epistle to the Hebrews.*

XIV.

THE INVOCATION OF SAINTS.

"There is . . . one mediator between God and men, the man Christ Jesus."—1 TIM. ii. 5.

THE sole mediation of our Lord Jesus Christ between man and God is the cardinal truth of Christianity, and the one great necessary condition of eternal salvation for our race. Through Him alone we know the Divine Father. Through His one sacrifice and oblation once offered we obtain the forgiveness of our sins. Through Him alone we have access to God in prayer. His words alone are our supreme oracle and law. He alone is the Way, the Truth, and the Life. No man cometh unto the Father but by Him. Through Him alone we know of the gift and power of the Divine Spirit. In Him alone we have eternal life.

With Him we need no mediator. "Come unto Me," He said, "all ye that labour and are heavy laden, and I will give you rest."[1] "All that the Father giveth Me shall come to Me; and he that cometh to Me I will in nowise cast out."[2] "My sheep hear My voice,

[1] Matt. xi. 28.   [2] John vi. 37.

and I know them, and they follow Me: and I give unto them eternal life; and they shall never perish, neither shall any man pluck them out of My hand."[1] "Where two or three are gathered together in My Name, there am I in the midst of them."[2] "Whatsoever ye shall ask in My Name that will I do."[3] "If ye shall ask anything in My Name, I will do it."[4] "Whatsoever ye shall ask the Father in My Name, He will give it you."[5] "Hitherto ye have asked nothing in My Name: ask, and ye shall receive, that your joy may be full."[6] "I say not unto you that I will pray the Father for you: for the Father Himself loveth you, because ye have loved Me, and have believed that I came out from God."[7] "By Him we have access by faith into this grace wherein we stand."[8] "Through Him we both have access by one Spirit unto the Father."[9] "In Him we have boldness and access with confidence by the faith of Him."[10] "By the blood of Jesus we have boldness to enter into the holiest by a new and living way which He hath consecrated for us."[11] No access could be more untrammelled, direct, complete, full, and absolute. Sin is the only hindrance; and as to that we know from St. John that "if any man sin, we have an advocate with the Father, Jesus Christ the righteous, and He is the propitiation for our sins."[12] "The blood of Jesus

[1] John x. 28.
[2] Matt. xviii. 20.
[3] John xiv. 13.
[4] John xiv. 14.
[5] John xvi. 23.
[6] John xvi. 24.
[7] John xvi. 27.
[8] Rom. v. 2.
[9] Eph. ii. 18.
[10] Eph. iii. 12.
[11] Heb. x. 19.
[12] 1 John ii. 1.

Christ, God's Son, cleanseth us from all sin. If we say that we have no sin, we deceive ourselves, and the truth is not in us: if we confess our sins" to ourselves and to God, "He is faithful and just to forgive us our sins, and to cleanse us from all unrighteousness."[1] We may come straight to God and say, "Father, I have sinned against Heaven and before Thee, and am no more worthy to be called Thy son."[2] Even if we could find another advocate to plead for us with our Saviour, and even if we could make that advocate hear, the employment of such advocacy would be, on the one hand, unnecessary, and on the other disloyal. It would be unnecessary, because the love of Christ for us is Divine and perfect, and cannot be increased. "Who shall separate us from the love of Christ?"[3] Remember His own words: "I pray not for these alone, but for them also which shall believe on Me through their word; that they all may be one; as Thou, Father, art in Me, and I in Thee, that they also may be one in us. And the glory which Thou gavest Me I have given them: that they may be one, even as we are one: I in them, and Thou in Me, that they may be made perfect in one."[4] In virtue of our faith in our Saviour we are already partakers of the Divine nature, we already have the fellowship of the Father and the Son. "If any man love Me, he will keep My words: and My Father will love him, and we will come unto him, and make our abode

---

[1] 1 John i. 9.   [2] Luke xv. 19.
[3] Rom. viii. 35.   [4] John xvii. 20.

with him."[1] We need nothing more than that assurance. To that assurance nothing could be added by the prayers of her who was so highly favoured, nor of the glorious company of the Apostles, nor of the noble army of martyrs. For all of these, we may be certain some fitting work is found in the land of the blesssd; but in face of such Divine promises there is no room for intervention, mediation, intercession on their part between us and the Head of that body of which we, like them, are the members. The endeavour to engage such advocates would on the other hand be disloyal. It would be distrustful of that near, complete, unhindered love of which we have the pledge. It would be putting Christ further off instead of bringing Him near. "The righteousness which is of faith speaketh on this wise: Say not in thine heart, who shall ascend into heaven (that is, to bring Christ down from above) . . . but what saith it? The word is nigh thee, in thy mouth, and in thy heart; that is, the word of faith which we preach; that if thou shalt confess with thy mouth the Lord Jesus, and shalt believe in thine heart that God hath raised Him from the dead, thou shalt be saved."[2] It would be giving to a creature the honour, whether in a higher or a lower degree, which is alone due to the Creator. When the mother wished in her fond anxiety to take a part in the work of her Son on earth, He said to her, with quiet decision, "Woman, what have I to do with thee?"[3] When the priest of Jupiter would have done sacrifice at

[1] John xiv. 23. [2] Rom. x. 6. [3] John ii. 4.

Lystra unto the Apostles Paul and Barnabas, what did they say? "They rent their clothes, and ran in among the people, and said, Sirs, why do ye these things? We also are men of like passions with you."[1] When St. John fell in his vision at the feet of the glorified elder who was given to him as a guide through the courts of heaven, and would have worshipped him, "See thou do it not," said that majestic presence; "I am thy fellow-servant, and of thy brethren that have the testimony of Jesus. Worship God!"[2] And again an angelic being was showing him the River of Life; again St. John fell down to worship before his feet. Again the same solemn message was repeated, "See thou do it not: for I am thy fellow-servant, and of thy brethren the prophets."[3] Very earnestly does St. Paul warn his beloved Colossians against those who imagined other beings between themselves and their one Mediator: "Let no man beguile you of your reward in a voluntary humility, and worshipping of angels, intruding into those things which he hath not seen, vainly puffed up in his fleshy mind, and not holding to the Head, from which all the body by joints and bands having nourishment ministered, increaseth with the increase of God."[4]

In the Primitive Church it was always esteemed one of the strong arguments for the Divinity of our Saviour that He alone, in right of His Divine being, was to be worshipped. It was then an un-

[1] Acts xiv. 15.   [2] Rev. xix. 10.
[3] Rev. xxii. 9.   [4] Col. ii. 18.

doubted principle that no creature, how excellent soever, was to be worshipped with religious worship, but only the living and true God. Use this word however much you please in an ambiguous sense; speak of a man of worship; you mean merely a man whom you think worthy. Talk if you like of the worshipful the chancellor; you mean only that the office of the chancellor is worthy of all respect. But when you begin to address your prayers to a created being, then you are using a different idea altogether. As long as these two assertions stand good, that Christ was from the first worshipped with religious worship, and that nothing should receive that but only the living and true God, then the Arian and Socinian cannot evade that argument from antiquity. Once give religious worship, even if it be said to be in a low degree, to saints and angels, and that argument is wholly enervated and destroyed. Justin Martyr often draws the distinction in his Apologies between religious worship and human honour; he tells the emperors that the Christians worship only God, earthly rulers they cheerfully serve.[1] Tertullian, speaking of the Christians' prayers for the emperors and the peace of the world, said that they asked these things of the living and true God; and they could ask them of no other but Him, of whom they were sure to obtain them, because He alone was able to give them.[2] This was the answer which the martyrs gave to their judges

[1] Justin, Apol. ii. 63.   [2] Tertull. Apol. xxx.

when ordered to offer supplications to the emperors: if they had been allowed to give the same homage which a certain section of Christians now give to saints and angels, it might have been argued in the same way that they were not interfering with the supreme honour of God, and they might have escaped.[1] Such expressions are frequent in other early writers: Theophilus, Bishop of Antioch, Dionysius, Bishop of Alexandria, Irenæus, Clement of Alexandria, Origen, Cyprian, Lactantius, Athenagoras, Tatian.[2]

Not only that, but the Primitive Church repudiated the worship of saints and angels in particular, and distinctly condemned it as idolatry. When the Jews at Smyrna desired the heathen judge not to allow the Christians to carry off the body of Polycarp, lest they should leave their crucified Master and worship Polycarp instead, "this suggestion," answered the Church of Smyrna, "proceeded from pure ignorance, that we could neither forsake Christ nor worship any other. For we worship Him, as being the Son of God; but the martyrs, as the disciples and followers of the Lord, we love with a due affection, for their great love of their own King and Master; with whom we desire to be partners and fellow-disciples."[3] Listen to Origen: "The angels are ministering spirits, that bring the gifts of God to us; but there is no command in Scripture

---

[1] Bingham, "Eccl. Antiqu.," bk. xiii. chap. iii.
[2] See the reff., ibid.
[3] *Martyr. Polycarp. ap. Euseb.*, bk. iv. chap. xv.

to worship or adore them. For all prayers, supplications, intercessions, and giving of thanks are to be sent up to God by the great High Priest, the Living Word of God, who is superior to all angels."[1] And again:[2] "We must endeavour to please God alone, who is above all things, and labour to have Him propitious unto us; procuring His goodwill with piety and all kind of virtue. And if Celsus will yet have us to procure the goodwill of any others after Him that is God over all, let him consider that as when the body is moved, the shadow follows its motion; so in like manner, when we have God, who is over all, favourable to us, that we shall have all His friends, both angels and souls and spirits, favourable unto us also. For they have a fellow-feeling with them that are thought worthy to find favour from God. Neither are they only favourable . . . but they labour also with them that are willing to worship God over all, and are friendly to them, and sympathise with them, and pray with them. So that we may be bold to say that when men who with resolution purpose unto themselves the best things, do pray unto God, many thousands of the sacred powers are praying together with them, unspoken to, without invocation." It had been previously said by Irenæus[3] that the Church in his time, though she wrought many miracles for the benefit of men, yet did nothing by invocation of angels, but only by prayer

---

[1] Origen against Celsus, v. p. 233.   [2] Ibid., viii. p. 420.
[3] Irenæus, ii. 57.

to God and the Lord Jesus Christ. It was said by Athanasius,[1] "No man would pray to receive anything from the Father and the angels, or from any other of the creatures; neither would any man say, God and the angel give me this." And again he reminds the Arians that Peter the Apostle did forbid Cornelius, when he would have worshipped him, saying, "I myself also am a man. . . . Wherefore it belongs to God only to be worshipped. And this the angels may well know, that though they excel others in glory, yet they are all but creatures; and not in the number of those that are to be worshipped, but of those that worship the Lord."[2] St. Augustine, in his last days, uses strong expressions about the honour due to saints; but on the point of addressing supplications to them he is most distinct.[3] "Let not our religion," he says, "consist in the worship of dead men; because if they lived piously, they are not thought to be such as would desire that kind of honour; but would have Him to be worshipped by us by whose illumination they rejoice to have us partners with them in their merit. They are therefore to be honoured for imitation, not to be worshipped for religion." And again: "That which the highest angel worships, the same is to be worshipped by the meanest man. And this we are to believe, that the

---

[1] *Athan. Orat.* iv. *contra Arianos*, tom. i. p. 464.
[2] Ibid. iii. *contra Arianos*, p. 394.
[3] August *de Verâ Religione*, c. 55.

very greatest angels, and most excellent ministers of God, would have us worship one God with them. And therefore we honour angels with love, not with religious service. Neither do we build temples to them: for they desire not to be so honoured by us, because they know that we ourselves, when we are good, are temples of the Most High God." And Chrysostom exhorts his hearers not to rely on the intercession of others, but to go immediately to God themselves; giving them the example of the woman of Canaan, who was never the better for the Apostles' intercession; who entreated not Peter or James to beg for her, but went directly to Christ herself, and from Him received a better answer. So he adds, "There is no need of intercessors with God."[1] For three hundred years after Christ there cannot be produced out of the genuine writings of one ancient father one clear or pertinent testimony for the invocation of saints or angels.

It was in the fourth century, when the Church was recognised by the emperors, and no longer suffered the wholesome discipline of persecution, that she began to lose the simplicity of the Gospel. We begin to see the asserted superiority of the clergy over the laity, the undue exaltation of the episcopal order, the germs of the supremacy of the Roman See, the unwise privileges and exceptions of the clerical order, the practice of hunting gifts and legacies, the en-

[1] Compare Chrysostom, Hom. V. *in Coloss.*, and Hom. VII. and Hom. IX.

couragement of clerical celibacy as a state of higher sanctity, the fierceness and almost incredible extravagances of monasticism, the exaggerated devotion to the mother of our Lord. And it was in this century that we first find traces of the invocation of saints. There were two eminent and holy men in particular to whom the innovation is owing, Gregory Nazianzene and Basil.[1] The one founded his commendation of the practice on a spurious life of Cyprian which was afterwards authoritatively condemned; the other, in speaking of the forty martyrs of Cappadocia, says that those who were in difficulties fled to them. He may mean merely to profit by their example; but the words are ambiguous, and are an additional proof, if we needed any, of the danger of using rhetorical flourishes of doubtful meaning. And Chrysostom, in spite of the wholesome sentence I have quoted from him already, undoubtedly said, "He that is emperor standeth praying to the saints, to the tentmaker and fisherman, Peter and Paul, to intercede with God for him." St. Chrysostom was also a great rhetorician, and sometimes contradicted himself. To this we may gladly oppose the words of St. Augustine: "The emperor, at the tomb of Peter, prayeth not to Peter, but to God." The fourth century was full of the germs of errors contrary to the teaching of Holy Scripture, and against these unwholesome tendencies we have to be on our guard.

[1] Basil, *Oratio in Barlaam*, p. 139; Greg. Nazian., i. 449.

It was at this time that patron saints began to be selected. A martyr supposed to have a special interest in a place and its inhabitants was called their patron first in the latter half of this same fourth century. Ambrose is the earliest witness of the fact, when in 386 he calls Gervasius and Protasius the patrons of the orthodox at Milan.[1] The usage was much extended by the Gallican poet Paulinus.[2] It was taken up by another poet Prudentius;[3] then it began to spread. The possession of a relic was thought to give right to the patronage of the saint. About 600 A.D. Theodelinda built a church near Milan in honour of John the Baptist, that he might be an intercessor for her husband and children.[4] In the 5th century Leo the Great, Bishop of Rome, declared St. Peter and St. Paul to be the special patrons of Rome.[5] A great writer, Alcuin, in a subsequent age, informs us that St. Ambrose was the patron of Milan, the Theban legion the patrons of the Pennine Alps, Bishop Hilary at Poictiers, Bishop Martin at Tours, St. Denis and St. Germain at Paris, Remigius in Champagne, and the like.[6] It was about the sixth century that a church dedicated to St. Michael was built at

---

[1] Ambrose, *Epist.* xxii. 11; Expos. on St. Luke, x. 12.
[2] Paulinus, *Carm.* ii.; St. Felix, 26, and many other places; especially his *Notatitia*.
[3] Prudentius, Hymns *de Coronis*.
[4] Paulus Winnfridus, *de Gestis Langobard*, i. 22.
[5] Leo, "Sermons," 80, § 5.
[6] Alcuin., *Homil. de Nat. Willibrordi*, i.

Ravenna, the first in honour of the angels.[1] The earliest church dedicated to the Mother of our Lord was probably that on the top of the Esquiline Hill at Rome, built by Pope Liberius about the middle of the fourth century.[2] The solemn invocation of the Virgin for prosperity in state affairs stands recorded in the Acts of the Emperor Justinian;[3] and the great General Narses never ventured on a battle without some sign of her approval. In this extreme zeal to pay to the Mother of Jesus Christ that very excess of honour against which He Himself had warned His disciples, there mingled both a lower feeling of human nature, and a trace of that heathen element which, during the fourth century, began to infect many other usages of the Church. The idea of a female mediator, performing in a higher world offices akin to those labours of mercy and intercession which befit the feminine character on earth, was one which the mind of mankind was ready to receive; and, moreover, this idea of the blessed Mary was welcomed as a substitute for some other ideas that had been lost by the fall of polytheism with its host of female deities. The veneration of her, therefore, advanced rapidly, although it was not until a much later period that it reached its height.[4] The first who brought her name as an object of the public devotions of the Greek Church is noted by Nicephorus to have been Peter the Fuller, a presbyter of Bithynia, afterwards

[1] Ciampini, *Vet. Monum.*
[2] Smith's "Eccl. Hist.," p. 452.
[3] Codex i. 37, 1.
[4] Robertson, vol. i. p. 582.

the usurper of the see of Antioch, about the year 470 A.D.; who, though a branded heretic, invented four things very useful, as he said, to the Catholic Church, of which the last was that in every prayer the Mother of God should be mentioned, and her Divine name invoked. As for the Latin Church, it was not till 130 years later, in Gregory's time, that this innovation took place.

The pagan superstitions connected with growing departure from Scripture and the Primitive Church rapidly increased. Basil calls the saints helpers of prayer.[1] Leo exhorts the people of Rome to keep vigil in St. Peter's, "who will deign by his prayers to assist our supplications, and fastings, and alms-givings." Gregory[3] gives them the same description as Basil. Paulinus[4] tells of a rustic who had lost two oxen by theft, instead of pursuing the robbers, flying at once to the church of St. Felix, whom he declares responsible for their restoration. Theodoret says that Christians made a point of giving the appellations of the martyrs to their children, by that means procuring for them safety and guardianship. In other ways the pagan idea asserted itself. The active assistance in battle of some long-departed hero was the subject of many a Greek and Roman myth. Among the half converts of the fourth century there

---

[1] Orations on Barlaam, Mamas, &c.   [2] Leo, *Serm.* 84, § 2.
[3] *Greg. Nyss.*, iii. 578.   [4] Paulinus, *Carm.*
[5] Theodoret, *Græc. aff. Cur.*

could not fail to be many on whom these romantic traditions had made a deep impression, and we cannot be altogether surprised at their speedy reproduction under a Christian guise.[1] The patron martyr was regarded as a faithful ally, both in aggression and defence, of those who served him well. It is, in short, in the heathen fable that we discover the germ of the mediæval romance which culminated in the conversion of the Apostles into knights-errant. Still more alien from the spirit and faith of the Gospel was the dependence placed on the patron saint for protection from the consequences of sin, even at the day of judgment. At the earliest period of the worship of patrons this blasphemy occurs. Prudentius, the unfortunate poet, whom I have before quoted, actually declares that he desired to be placed on the left hand of the Judge, in order that the martyr Romanus may come to his rescue at that awful moment!—to such a pitch of impious extravagance, even at this early period, were men led by the incautious words and the improper license in which the Christian poets indulged.[2]

You cannot but have been struck by the extraordinary contrast between these pagan corruptions and the direct teaching of our Lord, His Apostles, and the Primitive Church. When once, with the Church of Rome, you have admitted the doctrines of Development and of Accommodation, there is no

[1] Dict. of Christian Antiquities, Article *Patron Saints*.
[2] Prudentius, *De Coronis*, x.

length of blindness and perversity, no labyrinth of contradictions, into which you will not be led. This day, I beseech you, turn aside once more from all these bewildering heresies, and throw yourself, heart and soul and mind, on the sole mediation of Christ your Saviour. Tell Him directly all your sins and sorrows, your hopes and fears. He is ever present in you to listen and to give grace and strength. He is the same yesterday, to-day, and for ever. He is as ready to hear your cry, as that of the disciples in the storm, or the blind men by the way, or the leper afar off, or the despairing woman who would but touch the hem of His garment. Oh, remember what the result of the small germ of their faith was to these poor people: "As many as touched Him were made perfectly whole."

And to our dear brothers of the Roman persuasion, to whom the unbroken development of the Church is of greater consequence than the plain teaching of the Son of God, and to whom the tradition of fifteen hundred years, whatever its origin, is very dear, we would say this: Oh, think once more of the way in which you are walking! Christ never guaranteed even His own disciples against error. They thought St. John would never die; they thought the Lord would come to judgment in their own lifetime. It is not only the authority of the body to which you belong that is of importance, but the accordance of the truth that you hold with the teaching of the Son of God. The Jewish Church were splendidly and magnificently continuous: they had Abraham to their father; yet they were wrong, and they crucified Christ. When you talk with such hope and confidence of converting us, is it not a duty of Christian humility, in the face of such strong contradictions as those of which you cannot but be aware, to ask yourselves whether you too may not have been misled? Mistakes have been made by all of us in our time, from the Apostles downwards. This access of pagan influences in the fourth century, is it not worth inquiry? Will you not this day join us, laying aside all prepossession and prejudice, in praying the Holy Spirit once more to take us into His own hands, and guide us into all truth?

XV.

MITRES.

"Peradventure, because they have not the crook and mitre, as the old bishops had, displeases them."—"Works of Pilkington, Bishop of Durham," p. 584.

It has been remarked by one of the most eminent of living naturalists that in a barbarous condition of human society it is the male who chiefly adorns himself; as social life improves, or arrives at its middle condition, both sexes alike are splendid in their apparel; but that when civilisation has advanced to the reasonable and reflective stage, the male divests himself of ornaments and colours, and leaves them to the female, who considers them the natural and fitting accompaniments of the beauty to which she always desires to lay claim.

In the time of the Apostles, Roman and Greek civilisation were far advanced, and the costume of men was extremely simple. In the early Church the ministers of the assemblies wore merely the dress of ordinary life, and no doubt the soberest and most decent that they could command. It was only as civilisation began to decline and fashions to change that reverence began to be paid to the obsolete costumes which the clergy, by force of habit and by aversion to change, continued to wear.[1] As the intellectual elevation of the days of Greek and Roman culture continued to fade into the past in the time of the later empire, attention began to be paid to these details, as if they were part of religion. Rich and handsome garments of the particular shape on which the continual change of fashion had fixed the character of ecclesiastical were sent by devotees to bishops and presbyters; and as civilisation sank even farther into the dark ages, these increased in pagan splendour.

The revival of the obsolete and unauthorised mitre, part of the gorgeous paraphernalia of the centuries of superstition, by the present eminent and beloved Bishop of Lincoln in 1885, as one of the stages in the march of the Oxford movement, and the fact that his example has been already followed by six other exalted occupants of English sees, makes it desirable to look into the history of this strange adornment.

The mitre is first mentioned amongst ecclesiastical vestments in the middle of the eleventh century, though some kind of decorative episcopal head-gear had been in use considerably earlier.[2] It was first made of embroidered linen, and it does not appear in its

---

[1] Compare "Dictionary of Christian Antiquities," *Dress*; Stanley's "Christian Institutions," &c.
[2] Leo IX., *Epist.* 3; *Patrol. Lat.*, cxliii. 595.

well-known double or cleft form until the twelfth century had made considerable advance, when it began to be constructed of some rich material, and to be adorned with gold and jewels.[1] It was in the fourteenth century, when ladies' head-dresses became very high, that this peculiar and bizarre object attained its full development. Previously mitres were very low and concave in contour.

The words used for it in Latin and Greek are *mitra* and *infula*.[2] *Mitra* is a cap worn by women. Isidore of Seville, in his "Etymology," says, "It is a Phrygian cap protecting the head, such as is the ornament of devout women. The head-covering of men is called *pileum*, the head-covering of women *mitra*." It was also worn by Asiatics without distinction of sex. Mitra was thus the cap of women and effeminate men. Its prototype, the Phrygian cap, came into startling prominence at the time of the French Revolution. *Infula*, on the contrary, was the fillet which decked the head of heathen priests and victims. Servius defines it as "a garland, like a circular diadem, from which ribbons hang down on each side. It is usually broad and twisted of white and purple." Virgil often mentions the sacrificing priest wearing this garland. Victims about to be sacrificed, whether beasts or men, were tricked out with

---

[1] Cutts, "Dictionary of the Church of England," *Mitre*.
[2] This paper is throughout indebted to Mr. Sinker's article in the "Dictionary of Christian Antiquities."

the same ribbons. We have a gladiator in Suetonius, who, having been guilty of cowardice, was ornamented with a garland on being led to execution.

The earliest alleged instance of some sort of head-dress as part of the official costume of the Christian ministry is really only a metaphorical expression, and has nothing to do with the question. The passage occurs in a letter of Polycrates, Bishop of Ephesus, to Victor, Bishop of Rome (A.D. 192-202), on the subject of the Easter controversy (Euseb., "Hist. Eccl.," v. 24; also partly in iii. 31; cf. also Jerome, "De Viris Illustribus," c. 45), in which Polycrates cites the names of different Asiatic bishops and martyrs who are claimed as having held to the Asiatic practice. Amid this enumeration we read: "Yea, moreover, John too, he who lay on the Lord's breast, who became a priest wearing the golden plate (ὅς ἐγενήθη ἱερεύς, τὸ πέταλον πεφορεκώς), and a witness and teacher, he sleepeth in Ephesus." A somewhat parallel instance may be quoted from a later writer, Epiphanius. The reference has been to Christ as heir to the throne of David, which is a throne not only of royalty, but of priesthood. The Saviour thus stands at the head of a line of high-priests; James, the Lord's brother, being, as it were, successor, in virtue of his apparent relationship, and thus becoming Bishop of Jerusalem and president of the Church. Then follows a very extraordinary sentence, which can by no possibility be taken literally, unless it is a sheer mistake: "Moreover also, we find that he exercised the priestly office after the manner of the old priesthood; wherefore also it was permitted to him once in the year to enter into the Holy of Holies, as the law commanded the high-priests, according to the Scripture. Further, it was permissible for him to wear the golden plate upon his head (ἀλλὰ καὶ τὸ πέταλον ἐπὶ τῆς κεφαλῆς ἐξῆν αὐτῷ φέρειν), as the above-mentioned trustworthy writers have testified" ("Hær.," xxix. 4; vol. i. 119, ed. Petavius).

Mr. Sinker, the librarian of Trinity College, Cambridge, to whose article on the subject, in the "Dictionary of Christian Antiquities," I have already acknowledged my debt, points out that the question must mainly turn on the words of Polycrates, whose position, both in date and locality, would give his words more importance than those of Epiphanius. The probability lies strongly on the side of the language being viewed as allegorical. The passage in general has that character (cf. μεγαλα στοιχεῖα κεκοίμηται), and the perfect participle could hardly refer to a habit. Polycrates clearly aims at bringing out in a pointed and picturesque way the fact of the supreme apostolic authority of St. John, whose office in the Christian Church was to bear rule in spiritual things over the spiritual Israel, even as the high-priest of old over Israel after the flesh. This is the view of Marriott in the "Vestiarium Christianum." Epiphanius is no doubt referring loosely to the words of Polycrates;

that James could have been admitted as high-priest into the Holy of Holies of the Temple at Jerusalem is simply an impossibility. One thing, at any rate, Mr. Sinker considers plain enough. Even if the interpretation be not allegorical, and even if so remarkable a statement is to be taken as a matter of fact without any other evidence whatsoever, it would in any case have been an ornament special to St. John, or St. James, or both of them, and ceased with them, affecting in no sense the further use of the Church.

The metaphorical sense of Polycrates and Epiphanius is emphasised by the language of the oration delivered by Eusebius on the consecration of the great church at Tyre ("Hist. Eccl.," x. 4). This highly rhetorical discourse begins with an address to Paulinus, Bishop of Tyre, and his assembled clergy, as "friends of God and priests ($\iota\epsilon\rho\epsilon\hat{\iota}s$), who are clad in the holy robe that reacheth to the feet, and with the heavenly crown ($\sigma\tau\acute{\epsilon}\phi\alpha\nu\text{o}\nu$) of glory, and with the unction of inspiration ($\tau\grave{o}$ $\chi\rho\hat{\iota}\sigma\mu\alpha$ $\tau\grave{o}$ $\check{\epsilon}\nu\theta\epsilon\text{o}\nu$), and with the priestly vesture of the Holy Ghost." These words are an exact parallel to St. Paul's description of the Christian armour. They are no more to be taken literally in the one case than the other. Hefele, who argues for the early use of the mitre, does not suppose that $\sigma\tau\acute{\epsilon}\phi\alpha\nu\text{o}s$, even if taken literally, could mean more than the tonsure, which often went by this name.

Another poetical passage of the same character occurs in one of the discourses of St. Gregory Nazianzene (died A.D. 389), where he addresses his father, then Bishop of Nazianzus, who sought to associate his son with him in the duties of his office. He remarks: " Thou anointest the chief priest and clothest him with the robe reaching to the feet, and settest the priests' cap (τόν κίδαριν, one of the Septuagint words for the head-dress of priest and high-priest) about his head, and bringeth him to the altar of the spiritual burnt-offering, and sacrificest the calf of consecration, and dost consecrate his hands with the Spirit, and dost bring him into the Holy of Holies" ("Orat.," x. 4; " Patrol. Græc.," xxxv. 829). There is no reason why one of these expressions should arbitrarily be taken as literal, while the burnt-offering, the calf, the hands, and the Holy of Holies are metaphorical.

Another passage, which is sometimes misinterpreted, is from a heathen writer, Ammonianus Marcellinus. He describes (xxix. 5) the outbreak of an African chief, Firmus (A.D. 372). Against him is sent Theodosius, afterwards emperor. Firmus is compelled to sue for peace. The pagan historian describes the sending of " Christiani ritus antistites oraturos pacem." Two days afterwards Firmus restores " Icosium oppidum . . . militaria signa et coronam sacerdotalem cum cœteris quæ interceperat." This was clearly the golden crown worn by heathen priests (cf. Tertullian, " De Spectaculis," c. 23; " De Idololatria," c. 18; " De Corona Militis," c. 10). The evidence of the Council of Elvira on the wearing of the crown by heathen priests is very curious. One of its canons ordains that "(those who have been heathen) priests who only wear the crown, and do not perform sacrifices, nor contribute from their own funds to the expenses of the sacrifices, may be admitted to communion after two years" ("Concil. Illib.," can. 55; "Labbe," i. 976).

The use of the word *infula* has similarly been misunderstood. In classical usage it came to mean any ornaments or insignia of magistrates, and even the magistracy itself. In later ecclesiastical Latin it is used for a chasuble. In the absence of evidence pointing the other way, Mr. Sinker remarks that the natural explanation of the early use of the Christian *infula* is that the word betokens in a poetical or rhetorical sense the official dress, or hardly more than the quasi-official position of ordained persons. The Christian poet Prudentius, dwelling on the names of famous martyrs connected with Saragossa, says ("Peristeph.," iv. 79):

> "Hic sacerdotum domus infulata
> Valeriorum,"

where the reference is to Valerius, Bishop of Saragossa. The meaning is, "Here is the family of the Valerii, adorned with the episcopate." The whole poem is written in a highly wrought strain of metaphor, and is a palpable imitation of classical imagery.

There are other passages where the word *infula* is used in a classical way of episcopal authority.

Gelasius (died A.D. 496) speaks of certain characteristics in a person rendering him "clericalibus infulis reprobabilem"—episcopal authority ("Epist. ix., ad episc. Lucaniæ," Patrol., lix. 51). A biography of Willibald, a disciple of St. Boniface, speaking of his consecration, says: "Sacerdotalis infulæ ditatus erat honore"—endowed with episcopal authority (c. xi., Canisius, "Thesaurus," ii. 116). In a biography of Burckhardt, of Würzburg, another disciple of St. Boniface (written probably two hundred years after his time), he is spoken of as "pontificali infula dignus"—worthy of episcopal authority; and the Pope of the day is said to be "summi pontificatus infulæ non incongruus."

There is absolutely no weight in two other passages. Ennodius, a poet of the fifth century, says of St. Ambrose:

"Serta redimitus gestabat lucida fronte,
Distinctum gemmis ore parabat opus"—

"He wore shining garlands on his brow, and the work of his mouth was glorious with gems." It is a poetical passage speaking of his noble appearance and his brilliant eloquence. And Theodulf of Orleans (died A.D. 821), contrasting a Jewish high-priest with the spiritual character of the Christian minister, says:

"Illius ergo caput resplendens mitra tegebat :
Contegat et mentem jus pietasque tuum"—

"'The Jewish high-priest's head was covered with a spendid mitre; and so may your mind be covered by justice and piety."

None of these passages really point to a Christian head-dress. On the contrary, Tertullian asks: "Quis denique patriarches . . . quis vel postea apostolus aut evangelista aut *episcopus* invenitur coronatus?"— "What patriarch, what apostle, or evangelist, or bishop is ever found with a crown on his head?" ("De Corona Militis," c. 10). This ought to settle the question. The remains of Christian art furnish no evidence whatever for the use of such a head-dress, but distinctly point the other way. We have every reason to agree with Menard that "vix ante annum post Christum natum millesimum mitræ usum in ecclesiâ fuisse" ("Greg. Sacr.," 557). Menard justly insists on the fact that in numerous liturgical monuments (*e.g.*, a Mass for Easter day in the Cod. Ratoldi, before A.D. 986, where the ornaments of a Bishop are severally gone through), as well as in early writers who have fully entered into the subject of Christian vestments, as Rabanus Maurus, Amalarius, Walafrid Strabo, Alcuin (Pseudo-Alcuin), there is no mention whatever of a mitre.

Mr. Sinker will pardon the free use that has been made of his article in view of the practical importance of the subject. The first indisputable mention of a mitre is in A.D. 1049, when Archbishop Eberhard of Treves was at Rome, and Pope Leo. XI. placed on his head, in St. Peter's, on Passion Sunday, the Roman mitre: "Romanâ mitrâ caput vestrum insignivimus, qua et vos et successores vestri in ecclesiasticis officiis Romano more semper utaminî"—"We have decorated you with the Roman mitre, so that in virtue of it you and your successors may always employ the Roman usage in ecclesiastical affairs" (Epist. iii., Patrol. cxliii. 595). It is a Roman ornament, introduced in a corrupt age. It is rightly associated in the minds of the people of England with superstition, error, and tyranny. Heraldically it is a symbol of dignity, like the coronet or the helmet: for peers to wear their coronets, and knights and gentlemen their helmets, whenever they are on official duty, would be as reasonable as the revival of this obsolete Roman adornment. By declaring what the dress of a bishop should be, the Prayer-book has declared what it should not. May we not humbly hope that the seven august and venerated personages, who in deference perhaps to the contemporary taste for antiquarian and mediæval decoration, have adopted it, will gradually lay aside what can hardly be considered consistent with the simplicity that is in Christ?

www.ingramcontent.com/pod-product-compliance
Lightning Source LLC
Chambersburg PA
CBHW031941230426
43672CB00010B/2007